W9-AKD-908

The Persian Gulf War

by Don Nardo

America's
★★★★★WARS

Lucent Books, P.O. Box 289011, San Diego, CA 92198-0011

Books in the America's Wars Series:

The Revolutionary War

The Indian Wars

The War of 1812

The Mexican-American War

The Civil War

The Spanish-American War

World War I

World War II: The War in the Pacific

World War II: The War in Europe

The Korean War

The Vietnam War

The Persian Gulf War

Library of Congress Cataloging-in-Publication Data

Nardo, Don, 1947-
  The Persian Gulf War / by Don Nardo.
    p. cm. — (America's wars)
  Includes bibliographical references and index.
  Summary: An account of the war between the United Nations allies and Iraq from Saddam's military buildup to the cease-fire.
  ISBN 1-56006-411-0
  1. Persian Gulf War, 1991—Juvenile literature. [1. Persian Gulf War, 1991.] I. Title. II. Series.
DS79.72.N37   1991
956.704 3—dc20

91-23064
CIP
AC

Contents

Foreword

War, justifiable or not, is a descent into madness. George Washington, America's first president and commander-in-chief of its armed forces, wrote that his most fervent wish was "to see this plague of mankind, war, banished from the earth." Most, if not all of the forty presidents who succeeded Washington have echoed similar sentiments. Despite this, not one generation of Americans since the founding of the republic has been spared the maelstrom of war. In its brief history of just over two hundred years, the United States has been a combatant in eleven major wars. And four of those conflicts have occurred in the last fifty years.

America's reasons for going to war have differed little from those of most nations. Political, social, and economic forces were at work which either singly or in combination ushered America into each of its wars. A desire for independence motivated the Revolutionary War. The fear of annihilation led to the War of 1812. A related fear, that of having the nation divided, precipitated the Civil War. The need to contain an aggressor nation brought the United States into the Korean War. And territorial ambition lay behind the Mexican-American and the Indian Wars. Like all countries, America, at different times in its history, has been victimized by these forces and its citizens have been called to arms.

Whatever reasons may have been given to justify the use of military force, not all of America's wars have been popular. From the Revolutionary War to the Vietnam War, support of the people has alternately waxed and waned. For example, less than half of the colonists backed America's war of independence. In fact, most historians agree that at least one-third were committed to maintaining America's colonial status. During the Spanish-American War, a strong antiwar movement also developed. Resistance to the war was so high that the Democratic party made condemning the war a significant part of its platform in an attempt to lure voters into voting Democratic. The platform stated that "the burning issue of imperialism growing out of the Spanish war involves the very existence of the Republic and the destruction of our free institutions." More recently, the Vietnam War divided the nation like no other conflict had since the Civil War. The mushrooming antiwar movements in most major cities and colleges throughout the United States did more to bring that war to a conclusion than did actions on the battlefield.

Yet, there have been wars which have enjoyed overwhelming public support. World Wars I and II were popular because people believed that the survival of America's democratic institutions was at stake. In both wars, the American people rallied with an enthusiasm and spirit of self-sacrifice that was remarkable for a country with such a diverse population. Support for food and fuel rationing, the purchase of war bonds, a high rate of voluntary enlistments, and countless other forms of voluntarism, were characteristic of the people's response to those wars. Most recently, the Persian Gulf War prompted an unprecedented show of support even though the United States was not directly threatened by the conflict. Rallies in support of U.S. troops were widespread. Tens of thousands of individuals, including families, friends, and well-wishers of the troops sent packages of food, cosmetics, clothes, cassettes, and suntan oil. And even more supporters wrote letters to unknown soldiers that were forwarded to the military front. In fact, most public opinion polls revealed that up to 90 percent of all Americans approved of their nation's involvement.

The complex interplay of events and purposes that leads to military conflict should be included in a history of any war. A simple chronicling of battles and casualty lists at best offers only a partial history of war. Wars do not spontaneously erupt; nor does their memory perish. They are driven by underlying causes, fueled by policymakers, fought and supported by citizens, and remembered by those plotting a nation's future. For these reasons wars, or the fear of wars, will always leave an indelible stamp on any nation's history and influence its future.

The purpose of this series is to provide a full understanding of America's wars by presenting each war in a historical context. Each of the twelve volumes focuses on the events that led up to the war, the war itself, its impact on the home front, and its aftermath and influence upon future conflicts. The unique personalities, the dramatic acts of courage and compassion, as well as the despair and horror of war are all presented in this series. Together, they show why America's wars have dominated American consciousness in the past as well as how they guide many political decisions of today. In these vivid and objective accounts, students will gain an understanding of why America became involved in these conflicts, and how historians, military and government officials, and others have come to understand and interpret that involvement.

Chronology of Events

c. 1000 B.C.
First kingdom of Israel flourishes in Palestine.

c. 600 B.C.
Babylonian Empire flourishes in Iraq.

A.D. 570
Prophet Muhammad born.

622
Muhammad flees Mecca for Medina, Islamic calendar begins.

1096–1303
Crusades fought in Palestine between Christians and Moslems.

1897
Theodor Herzl organizes first Zionist congress in Switzerland.

1914–1918
World War I fought.

1917
British issue Balfour Declaration endorsing the establishment of a Jewish state in Palestine.

1928
U.S. oil companies begin drilling in Iraq.

1932
Britain grants Iraq independence.

1939–1945
World War II fought.

1945
Arab League founded.

1948
State of Israel declared, first Arab-Israeli war fought.

1956
Suez Canal crisis, second Arab-Israeli war fought.

1961
Britain grants Kuwait independence.

1965–1973
Vietnam War fought.

1967
Third Arab-Israeli war fought.

1973
Fourth Arab-Israeli war fought, Arabs cut off oil to West.

1979
Saddam Hussein becomes president of Iraq.

1980–1988
Iraq-Iran war fought.

1988
George Bush is elected president of the United States.

1990
August 2 Iraq invades Kuwait.
August 7 President Bush orders U.S. troops to Saudi Arabia.
November 29 United Nations approves use of force to get Iraq to leave Kuwait.

1991
January 9 Meeting in Switzerland between Americans and Iraqis fails to bring peace.
January 15 U.N. deadline for Iraq to leave Kuwait.
January 16 Allied air forces attack Iraq and occupied Kuwait.
February 13 U.S. accidentally bombs Iraqi bomb shelter, killing more than 400.
February 23 Allied ground forces assault Iraq and Kuwait.
February 27–28 Kuwait is liberated, fighting ceases.
March 3 Allied commanders meet with Iraqis and dictate cease-fire terms.

INTRODUCTION

Renewal

The world was stunned on August 2, 1990, by alarming news. The Middle Eastern country of Iraq, led by President Saddam Hussein, had suddenly invaded Kuwait, its much smaller neighbor. In only three days, more than 100,000 Iraqi troops took control of Kuwait's capital, Kuwait City, seized the country's rich oil fields, and forced the Kuwaiti royal family into exile. For months, heads of state and diplomats from many countries tried to persuade Saddam to remove his troops. His continued refusals finally convinced the United States and the United Nations to use military force against Saddam. The war that ensued was short and decisive. On January 16, 1991, U.S. and other U.N.-sponsored forces destroyed

A U.S. Marine strains to hoist a shell for a 155mm howitzer during artillery fire against an Iraqi position near Kafji, Saudi Arabia.

Israeli troops capture the Arab section of Jerusalem in 1967.

Iraq's industrial and war-making facilities, crushed the Iraqi army, and liberated Kuwait in just forty-three days.

Though the war was short, its effects on the United States, the Middle East, and the world were significant. In the United States, success in the Gulf War sparked renewed feelings of pride and confidence among Americans. Before the war began, many in the United States had worried that the country might become involved in another long, costly, and unpopular war like the Vietnam conflict of the 1960s and 1970s. Addressing these worries, President George Bush said, "In our country, I know that there are fears of another Vietnam. Let me assure you, should military action be required, this will not be another Vietnam. This will not be another protracted, drawn-out war." After the war's successful conclusion, worries of another Vietnam ended. As one U.S. Army officer declared proudly, "The stigma [disgrace] of Vietnam has been erased."

The Gulf War was also significant for the people of the Middle East. For decades, most of the tension and fighting in the region had been between the Arab countries and Israel. Most Arabs were united in their hatred for Israel and their distrust of foreign powers that backed the Israelis, including the United States. Saddam Hussein's takeover of Kuwait was the first instance ever over which Arab countries joined foreigners to fight other Arabs.

The Gulf War also marked another important first. Never before in its forty-five-year history had the United Nations taken such a tough political and military stand against a country's naked aggression. Many people felt that the United Nations was at last fulfilling the function for which it had been created—to ensure that the nations of the world live in peace. The United Nations' strong response to Iraq's invasion sent a clear signal to all countries that the world community is not likely to tolerate such aggressions in the future.

CHAPTER ONE

The Middle East—
The Desert Sows
the Seeds of Crisis

For centuries, the Middle East has been one of the most important, argued about, and fought over areas in the world. One reason for this is the Middle East's strategic location. Since it lies at the crossroads of three continents—Europe, Asia, and Africa—people of these continents' nations had to pass through the Middle East to establish trade and military routes. To protect these routes, other nations conquered and controlled Middle Eastern countries.

Struggles over Land and Self-Rule

During most of the centuries that foreign powers controlled the Middle East, the native peoples of the area had little or no control over the land. A majority of the natives were Arabs, seminomadic people descended from ancient Semitic tribes. Even as late as the beginning of the twentieth century, Arab people belonged to many small tribes scattered across the Middle East. Most lived in tents and made their livings by herding, trading, or fishing. These tribes often warred and fought one another over land, water, and countless other issues. At that time, the Turks, who ruled a large, powerful empire centered in Turkey south of the Black Sea, controlled much of the Middle East. Even though Arabs were unhappy with Turkish rule, they could only dream of driving out the Turks. The Turks were powerful. As long as the Arabic tribes remained divided, the Turks easily controlled the area. This situation changed dramatically during World War I.

The Crusades

The Crusades were a series of holy wars waged by the Christian kingdoms of Europe against the Moslems of the Middle East. There were eight major and a number of minor Crusades between 1096 and 1303. Pope Urban II called for the First Crusade to free the holy city of Jerusalem from Moslem control. For centuries, Moslem leaders had allowed Christian pilgrims to visit the city's shrines. But in the year 1055, the Seljuk Turks, a warlike people from the region south of the Black Sea, took control of Palestine. The Turks, who were fanatic Moslems, restricted Christian access to Jerusalem. Responding to the pope's call, several French and Italian armies marched across Europe and invaded Palestine. They retook Jerusalem on July 15, 1099, and proceeded to massacre thousands of Moslem and Jewish civilians.

During the following two centuries, control over Jerusalem passed back and forth between Christians and Moslems several times. Armies from England, Germany, Hungary, and other Christian states took part in various expeditions to the holy lands. Perhaps the most famous Crusade was the Third, in which England's Richard I, the "Lionheart," faced off against the great warrior-statesman Saladin. Their conflict ended largely in a stalemate.

Although the campaigns were initially inspired by religious zeal, the Crusaders soon found other motives for the expeditions. In particular, the wars opened up valuable trade routes between Europe and the lands of the Near and Far East. Spices, sugar, fruits, drugs, perfumes, rugs, jewelry, glass, and fine steel products flowed into European castles and shops. This commerce helped the growth of local economies and stimulated the development of banking practices. In general, the Crusades aided the financial and cultural growth of Europe.

By contrast, the Moslems suffered as a result of the Crusades. Christian armies treated Moslems harshly, often raping the women and wiping out whole villages. The Europeans ridiculed Islam and purposely destroyed Moslem art, literature, and culture. As a result, Moslems distrusted the Western Christian nations and became less tolerant of foreigners and non-Moslems. This attitude, along with bitter memories of the Crusades, persists in the Middle East.

Medieval Crusaders salute the "true" cross as they march to battle Moslem forces in Palestine.

The Middle East

GREECE
TURKEY
SOVIET UNION
SOVIET UNION
Caspian Sea
MEDITERRANEAN SEA
LEBANON
ISRAEL
SYRIA
JORDAN
IRAQ
IRAN
AFGHANISTAN
LIBYA
EGYPT
KUWAIT
QATAR
PERSIAN GULF
SAUDI ARABIA
PAKISTAN
UNITED ARAB EMIRATES
OMAN
RED SEA
CHAD
SUDAN
YEMEN
INDIAN OCEAN
SCALE OF MILES
0   200   400
ETHIOPIA
SOMALIA

The Middle East, often referred to as the Near East, is the general name for the territories east and southeast of the Mediterranean Sea. Syria, Iraq, and Iran are the northernmost nations in the region. Farther south are Lebanon, Israel, Jordan, Kuwait, and Saudi Arabia. Clustered around the southern end of the Arabian peninsula are several small Arab countries, including North and South Yemen and Oman. Egypt and Libya, located across the Red Sea in North Africa, are also considered parts of the Middle East. The eastern Mediterranean, the Red Sea, and the Persian Gulf, which borders the Arabian peninsula in the east, are the vital waterways supporting the region.

During that war, the British, French, Americans, and their allies fought against the Germans and their allies, including the Turks. The British and French wanted to force the Turks out of the Middle East to reduce and weaken the Turkish Empire. They also wanted to control the Middle East after the war. In 1916, the British succeeded in briefly uniting the Arab tribes and organizing a revolt against the Turks. This marked the first time in centuries that the tribes had achieved any kind of unity. British leaders were successful because they promised that if the Arabs helped defeat the Turks, Britain would allow them to establish their own nations in the region.

Aided by the Arabs, the British, French, and their allies were able to drive the Turks out of the Middle East. Britain and France, the two most powerful European nations, controlled the area at the close of World War I. The Arabs expected to receive their reward—the right to set up their own countries. But Britain and France did not keep their promise to the Arabs. Instead the two European nations divided most of the Middle East into separate territories. They administered these territories under their own mandates, or rights to govern. They assured Arab leaders that various parts of the region would be granted independence in the future when the British and French believed the time was right. The Arabs protested, but it was no use. Although they had achieved temporary unity, the Arabs lacked the wealth and military power needed to stand up to the Europeans. This setback created a great deal of Arab resentment against all European nations, especially Britain and France.

These resentments increased in 1922. Britain and France had used their status as powerful nations to impose their mandates

Zionism

Palestine was the ancient home of the Jewish people. It was there that the original state of Israel, the kingdom of David and Solomon, thrived some three thousand years ago. Over the course of the centuries, the Jews were scattered around the world. But the return to Zion, to Jerusalem and the holy lands, remained an important part of Jewish tradition.

In 1882, a small group of European Jews adopted the name Lovers of Zion and founded a community in Palestine. They hoped that other Jews from around the world would follow their lead and return to the land of their ancestors. A few years later, Theodor Herzl, an Austrian journalist, published *The Jewish State*. In the book, Herzl argued that Jews were considered outsiders in every nation and continually suffered persecution. Only by forming their own nation, he said, could they live with complete freedom and dignity. In 1897, Herzl organized the first Zionist congress in Switzerland. The official goal of the organization was "to create for the Jewish people a home in Palestine secured by public law."

During World War I, the British endorsed the Zionists. In 1917, the British issued the Balfour Declaration, committing Britain to helping the Jews find a homeland.

on the people of the Middle East. But these mandates would not be official in the eyes of the world community until approved by the League of Nations, an international organization set up after World War I. When the British and French sought this official approval, the league upheld the mandates. The league gave permission for Britain and France to develop the Middle Eastern territories as they saw fit until they deemed these lands ready for independence. Britain retained control of Iraq, Jordan, and Palestine, the area bordering the eastern shores of the Mediterranean Sea. France continued to administer Syria, which included what would later become Lebanon.

The Zionist Factor

Arab resentment also centered around another issue in which Britain was involved. The British wanted to set up a Jewish homeland in Palestine. During World War I, to get Jewish support for the war effort, the British began supporting a group of European Jews known as Zionists. The Zionists believed that Jews should be allowed to rule their own country in the Palestinian lands that their ancestors occupied in Biblical times. In support of the Zionists, the British issued the Balfour Declaration in 1917, announcing that Britain endorsed the idea of a Palestinian Jewish state. The document declared that establishing such a state should not threaten the civil and religious rights of non-Jewish peoples in the region.

When the League of Nations approved the British mandate for Palestine in 1922, it also approved the Balfour Declaration. Many Western nations, including the United States, publicly supported the idea of a Jewish state in Palestine. These countries had large, influential Jewish communities that pressured their governments to support the Zionists. In response to the declaration, Jews from many parts of the world began emigrating to the Middle East, believing that the British would eventually grant them an independent nation.

But the Arabs strongly opposed the establishment of a Jewish state. They believed that since most of the people living in the area were Arab, Palestine was Arab land. They also felt that it was unfair that after having prevented the establishment of Arab nations, Western countries wanted to give the Jews an independent country in the Middle East. Most Arab leaders interpreted British support for a Jewish homeland as an attempt to gain a Western power base in the area. A Jewish homeland would allow the British to maintain influence in the region even after the Arabs gained their independence. Arab bitterness over Britain's pro-Zionist policies marked the beginning of the Arab-Jewish conflict that remains unresolved to this day.

The Rise of Islam

Religion has been a major source of tension and misunderstanding between Arabs and Westerners over the centuries. The Arabs practice Islam, a strict religion that helps shape their laws, family and social customs, and world views.

Practiced by more than 800 million people, Islam is the world's second largest religion after Christianity. Followers of Islam are called Moslems. They adhere to the teachings of the prophet Muhammad, who was born about the year A.D. 570 in Mecca, an Arabian town near the coast of the Red Sea. According to Moslems, Muhammad received a series of revelations, or messages, from God, whom the Arabs refer to as Allah. The content of these revelations became the basis for Islam's holiest book, the Koran.

Muhammad began teaching the principles of Islam, which include recognizing Allah as the one true God, submitting fully to God's will, and following strict moral rules. The new faith quickly gained converts. Fearing that Muhammad might become too powerful and upset the established order, local rulers began persecuting Moslems. In the year 622, Muhammad fled with seventy of his followers to Medina, a town some two hundred miles north of Mecca. Moslems mark his flight, called the Hegira, as the beginning of the Islamic calendar.

Muhammad succeeded in converting the population of Medina to Islam. In 630, he led a small army of Moslems in the conquest of Mecca and forced the residents to convert. Mecca and Medina soon became the holy cities of Islam. Muhammad advocated the concept of *jihad,* or violent struggle, to spread the faith to nonbelievers. After his death in 632, many of his followers interpreted jihad to mean "spreading the faith by military means," and the word came to mean "holy war." In the following years, Moslem armies conquered all the peoples of the Arabian peninsula. They then spread into what are now Palestine, Iraq, and Syria. By the year 717, Moslem armies controlled large portions of India and central Asia, as well as most of northern Africa and southern Spain.

Islam is partly based on the teachings and ideas of Judaism and Christianity. For instance, Moslems recognize large portions of the Old and New Testaments as holy books. They also recognize a long line of Christianity's prophets, including Adam, Abraham, Moses, and Jesus. Moslems believe that rejection of Islam is the same as rejection of God and is, therefore, the main cause of chaos and confusion in the world. According to the rules of the faith, Moslems must be charitable to the poor and pray five times each day while facing Mecca. They must also make a pilgrimage, or journey, to Mecca at least once during their lives.

The Quest for Buried Riches

Arabs were also bitter over Western nations' exploitation of the natural resources of the Middle East. Both Britain and France coveted Middle Eastern oil reserves. The Europeans still controlled the area and claimed the right to take as much oil as they wanted. Arabs believed that this oil belonged to them, but they lacked the money and expertise to extract the oil. Oil became one of the major reasons for fighting in the Middle East, between Arabs and Westerners and among the Arabs themselves. In fact, oil was a primary reason for Iraq's invasion of Kuwait in 1990.

In the 1920s, large Western nations like Britain and the United States became dependent upon Middle Eastern oil. Before World War I, the British produced less than 5 percent of the world's oil. When they took control of Iraq after the war, they gained some of the Middle East's largest oil fields and, by 1919, the British produced more than half of the world's oil.

The United States vigorously protested Britain's attempt to corner the world oil market. U.S. leaders argued that they had supplied Britain with oil during the war and deserved a fair share of oil supplies from the Middle East. After continued protests and negotiations, the British allowed five U.S. companies to operate in Iraq in 1928. In the following years, U.S. oil corporations expanded their operations into other Middle Eastern areas, including Kuwait. By 1938, the United States controlled more of the region's oil reserves than any other nation, and Americans increasingly relied on Middle Eastern oil. The need to protect these oil interests became an important reason for later U.S. intervention in Middle Eastern affairs, including the Gulf War against Iraq.

During the 1920s and 1930s, the Arabs felt compelled to cooperate with Western oil companies. The Arabs needed the advanced technical knowledge and oil equipment imported by the British and Americans. This situation remained largely unchanged until another world war altered the balance of power in the Middle East.

The Emergence of Arab Unity

During World War II, the old colonial empires of nations like France and Britain broke up. These countries had all they could do to fight the war and could no longer maintain so many far-flung colonies. Many of these colonies around the world gained their independence, including some in the Middle East. France, for example, granted independence to Syria in 1941 and Lebanon in 1943. By the closing days of the war in 1944, Britain was the only foreign power still occupying the Middle East. More and more Arabs demanded British withdrawal. It was in support of this purpose that Arab nations again achieved some unity.

On March 22, 1945, representatives from the seven independent Middle Eastern states met in Cairo, Egypt. Iraq, Egypt, Transjordan, Yemen, Saudi Arabia, Syria, and Lebanon established the Arab League, with the goal of working for the common interests of all Arabs. But personal rivalries and other differences between several of the member states prevented the new organization from reaching initial agreements. There was one topic, however, on which all seven members agreed. They were strongly opposed to a Jewish homeland in Palestine.

The establishment of a Jewish state became a major international issue following World War II. Millions of European Jews had been killed by the German Nazis, and hundreds of thousands of displaced Jews suffered in refugee camps. Many countries, including the United States, pressured Britain to withdraw from Palestine to allow these Jews to set up their own independently run nation. In 1947, the British finally gave in to the pressure and announced that they would withdraw from Palestine on May 15, 1948.

The United Nations, the world organization set up at the end of World War II, immediately began discussing what should be done about Palestine. After intense arguments and debates, the U.N. voted on November 29, 1947, to partition, or divide, Palestine

(below left) A young Jewish boy identified by the Star-of-David patch has a blanket smuggled to him by other inmates in one of the many Nazi concentration camps that imprisoned millions of Jews during World War II. (below right) Jewish refugees from Europe crowd the decks of a ship carrying them to their new homeland in Palestine in 1947.

The first prime minister of the newly declared state of Israel, David Ben-Gurion (left), watches as another Israeli official unrolls the document that declares Israel an independent nation.

into two states after the British pullout. One state would be Jewish, the other Arab, and both would share the capital city of Jerusalem, to be administered by the U.N. The Jews were elated. But the Arabs, still against the notion of a Jewish homeland, completely rejected the idea. The Arab League called for Arabs all over the Middle East to prevent the U.N. plan from going into effect. During the following months, there were many skirmishes, ambushes, and acts of terrorism between Arab and Jewish guerrilla armies in Palestine.

The Jewish Homeland Becomes a Reality

On May 14, 1948, the day before the final British evacuation, an announcement from Palestine electrified the world. David Ben-Gurion, leader of the Jewish forces, formally proclaimed the establishment of the nation of Israel. The Jews had decided to declare their independence before the U.N. officially granted it. By doing this, the Jews were able to postpone the U.N. decision to partition Palestine and had more control over the fate of Israel. The United States immediately recognized the new state. The Soviet Union and most other members of the United Nations also recognized it. Just as quickly, the members of the Arab

League declared war on Israel. Armies from six Arab nations marched into Palestine.

The resulting 1948 Arab-Israeli war lasted less than eight months. Even though the combined population of the Arab states was forty times larger than that of Israel, the Israelis won a resounding victory. In the war, Israeli forces succeeded in capturing some of the lands the U.N. had designated to the Arabs. In January 1949, Israel controlled 30 percent more territory than the U.N. had originally assigned it. Hundreds of thousands of Arabs who lived in the newly captured territories became refugees or had to live under Israeli authority. The problem of what to do about these displaced Palestinians has been an obstacle to Middle East peace ever since.

Angry and humiliated over their defeat, many Arabs criticized the United States for recognizing and supporting Israel during the 1948 war. Convinced that the United States would continue to back and strengthen Israel, several Arab nations turned to the Soviet Union for financial and military aid. The Soviets supplied the Arabs with both money and weapons. In order to counter Soviet influence in the region, as well as help Israel, the United States became more aligned with Israel and increasingly involved in Middle East affairs.

Jubilant Israeli children flock to buy the new flag of Israel after independent statehood is proclaimed in 1948.

(left) French and British naval forces approach Egypt's Port Said in 1956 to defend the Suez Canal against an Egyptian take-over. (right) Ships sunk by Egyptian forces form a barrier across the Suez Canal. The Egyptians hoped the barrier would slow the advance of the British and French navies which approach in the background.

The United States developed a Middle East policy that centered on four major goals. First, the United States dedicated itself to ensuring the security of Israel. This included supplying Israel with weapons and other military aid. Second, U.S. leaders vowed to work for an Arab-Israeli peace settlement. The third U.S. objective was to maintain American access to Middle Eastern oil, a vital commodity to the U.S. economy. Fourth, the United States sought to keep the Arabs from becoming too friendly with the Soviets.

Arab leaders often criticized U.S. goals as insincere and contradictory. For example, they accused the United States of caring more about Arab oil than they cared about the Arabs themselves. In addition, the Arabs insisted that the United States could not hope to bring peace to the region until it stopped backing Israel. Arab-American relations remained strained as more bloody conflicts continued to wrack the Middle East.

Arab Quarrels with Israel and the West

In the following years, the Arabs refused to accept Israel's right to exist and searched for ways to weaken and disrupt the Jewish state. In 1956, Egypt boldly took control of the Suez Canal. This important shipping route connecting the Mediterranean and Red seas was owned by Britain, France, and other European countries, and operated by Britain. The Egyptians refused to guarantee the safety of Israeli shipping, hoping to cut off supply lines to Israel. Israeli forces retaliated by attacking Egypt on October 29 and quickly fought their way toward the canal. The Egyptians soon found that they had to contend with more than just the Israelis. On November 5, British and French forces joined in the battle against the Egyptians and, by November 7, regained control of the canal.

Arabs and Israelis clashed again in 1967. Egypt moved troops toward the Israeli border and at the same time imposed a blockade on Israeli shipping. Other Arab countries began to mobilize their troops. Fearing they were about to be invaded from all sides, the Israelis attacked Egypt, Jordan, and Syria on June 5. Israeli jets destroyed the Egyptian air force while it was still on the ground. In just six days, Israel crippled the Arab armies and captured borderlands belonging to Syria and Jordan.

During the next six years, tensions in the Middle East remained high as the United States built up the Israeli military and the Soviet Union supplied arms to the Arabs. Carrying the fight beyond the Middle Eastern borders, Arab terrorists hijacked airplanes and attacked civilians in many parts of the world. The Arabs were determined to get back the lands they had lost in the previous wars and destroy Israel once and for all. On October 6, 1973, Arab armies launched a surprise attack on Israel. At first the Arabs gained some ground, but eventually the Israelis drove them back and once again defeated the Arabs.

(below left) Egyptian soldiers capture an Israeli defensive position during the 1973 war between Israel and Egypt. (below right) The 1973 Arab oil embargo against the United States caused long lines at filling stations.

Iraqi soldiers taunt captured Iranian POWs at the beginning of the eight-year war between Iran and Iraq.

U.S.-Arab relations became especially strained during the 1973 Arab-Israeli conflict. OPEC, or the Organization of Petroleum Exporting Countries, most of whose members are Arabs, wanted to pressure the United States into ceasing its support for Israel. A majority of OPEC members voted to raise the price of oil to levels four times higher than normal. OPEC also cut off oil supplies to the United States and several other countries. This oil embargo resulted in gas rationing and economic troubles for Americans. The United States did not give up its support for Israel, but it did work harder to negotiate settlements acceptable to both sides. Convinced that the United States would be more evenhanded in the future, the Arabs lifted the embargo in 1974.

Conflicts over Control of the Gulf

When the Arabs raised oil prices in the 1970s, some Middle Eastern countries grew wealthy. Iraq, Saudi Arabia, and Kuwait, which Britain granted independence in 1961, benefited enormously from growing oil profits. But the quest for wealth also created increased tensions among the oil-producing nations themselves. For instance, both Iraq and its eastern neighbor Iran wanted to control oil shipping in the Persian Gulf, the 650-mile-long bay that borders both countries. This rivalry reopened an old Iraqi-Iranian dispute.

Since the 1800s, Iraq and Iran had argued and fought over the Shatt al-Arab waterway on the northern edge of the Persian

Gulf. Vital to trade, the waterway was essential to the economies of both nations. In 1979, the dispute intensified, and each side threatened the other. On September 17, 1980, Iraq's president Saddam Hussein claimed complete control of the Shatt al-Arab and forbade ships flying the Iranian flag to enter. Five days later, Iraqi troops invaded Iran and destroyed key Iranian oil installations. The Iranians counterattacked, blowing up many Iraqi oil facilities.

The eight-year war that followed was the bloodiest yet seen in the Middle East. An estimated one million people died in the conflict. During the fighting, both sides launched missile attacks on cities and other civilian targets and used deadly chemical weapons on the battlefield. Neither Iraq nor Iran emerged from the war as a clear winner. When the U.N. negotiated a cease-fire in 1988, both countries controlled approximately the same territories they had at the beginning of the war.

The Iraq-Iran war put a huge financial strain on Iraq. During the conflict, Iraq built up the largest military force in the Middle East. The country used much of its vast oil wealth to buy missiles, tanks, artillery, and other weapons from France, the Soviet Union, the United States, and other nations. Iraq received additional money for weapons and other war supplies from rich Arab neighbors, Saudi Arabia and Kuwait in particular. In all, Iraq spent hundreds of billions of dollars buying weapons, waging war, and rebuilding destroyed oil facilities. By 1990, the country was heavily in debt, and Saddam Hussein desperately needed money. He wanted to find a way to eliminate Iraq's debts, expand the country's economy, and gain control of the Persian Gulf. The strategy he chose to achieve these goals would soon plunge his people and the peoples of other Middle Eastern nations into yet another disastrous war.

CHAPTER TWO

"We Will Make the Gulf a Graveyard"– Iraq Invades Kuwait

Ever since becoming leader of Iraq in 1979, Saddam Hussein's dream had been to restore Iraq to its former greatness. His goal was to use money from the country's oil industry to make Iraq a modern version of Babylon, the ancient capital of the mighty Babylonian Empire which had been centered in Iraq. Saddam even began rebuilding sections of Babylon's ruins to symbolize the power and glory of modern Iraq.

But it was his own image, not that of the Iraqi people, that Saddam sought to enhance. Saddam wanted to increase his prestige with all Arabs and exercise a controlling influence over the course of Middle Eastern affairs. He called himself the "Knight of the Arab Nation," the only leader strong and brave enough to unite all Arabs and stand up to Israel and its Western supporters. Many Arabs began to see him as their champion. Most Jordanians, for example, still bitter over their losses in the Arab-Israeli wars, strongly backed Saddam. And many Palestinian Arabs living in Israel praised Saddam. They believed that he supported their cause for a Palestinian homeland separate from Israel. The Palestine Liberation Organization, or PLO, an Arab group fighting to establish such a homeland, also embraced Saddam with enthusiasm.

Building Power and Prestige

During the 1980s, Saddam became a powerful leader in Iraq. To maintain his authority, Saddam ruled with an iron hand. According to Iraq's constitution, the nation is a republic, a state with a

Iraq—"The Land Between Rivers"

Iraq was one of the first places where human civilization grew and prospered. Most historians believe that the fertile valleys of Iraq's Tigris and Euphrates rivers supported widespread agriculture and organized communities over seven thousand years ago. There, the ancient Sumerian civilization grew and flourished. People built cities, made pottery, smelted metals, and recorded their language in writing. The region became known as Mesopotamia, or "the land between rivers." Eventually, the Babylonian Empire rose in the region and extended its control over much of the Middle East. Babylon, one of the greatest cities of the ancient world, was the home of the lush Hanging Gardens, one of the seven wonders of the world. Eventually, the Babylonian Empire weakened and fell, and a succession of foreign conquerors, including the Persians, Greeks, and Romans, occupied Iraq.

It was in the seventh century A.D. that Iraq came under the control of the fast-growing Arab empire founded by the prophet Muhammad. The people of the area converted to Islam, which remains Iraq's principal religion. Under the rule of the Arabs, Baghdad, Iraq's capital, became a wealthy and renowned center of learning, culture, science, and the arts. But the thirteenth-century invasion by the Mongols, a nomadic Asiatic people, caused the area to decline rapidly. During centuries of Mongol and later Turkish domination, most Iraqis were poor and illiterate. When Turkish rule ended during World War I, the British administered Iraq. The British granted Iraq independence in 1932 but continued to exert a strong influence on Iraqi affairs until the late 1950s.

After several bloody power struggles between rival Iraqi political factions in the 1960s, the Ba'ath party took control of Iraq. The Ba'athists are strongly pan-Arab, believing that all Arabs should unite against Israel and the Western nations. The Ba'athist leaders sought to control all aspects of Iraqi society. Saddam Hussein, who came to power in 1979, was no exception. He suppressed ethnic and language differences and tried to make his citizens adhere to Ba'athist beliefs and ideas. He often used the army and his own secret police to enforce his will on the people.

One of the seven wonders of the ancient world, the Hanging Gardens of Babylon, were located between the Tigris and Euphrates rivers in what is today Iraq.

national assembly run by representatives of the people. But after taking power, Saddam became a dictator. He exercised total control over the government, the army, the press, and the oil industry. Anyone daring to speak out against him was tortured and/or executed. Many Iraqi politicians, writers, and businesspeople fled to other countries to escape Saddam's tyranny. Saddam made sure that most of the money the country made from oil was used to support the military or ended up in his own bank accounts. Most of the Iraqi people, mainly merchants, farmers, herders, and laborers, remained poor.

As a way to extend his power and prestige beyond Iraq's borders, Saddam waged an eight-year campaign against Iran. He wanted to eliminate Iran as a competitor in the lucrative Persian Gulf oil industry to expand Iraq's wealth. Saddam also wanted to bolster his image with Arab nations who disliked Iran. Many Arabs, including the Kuwaitis and Saudis, looked upon the non-Arabic Iranians as a potential economic and military threat. Saddam reasoned that fighting the Iranians would increase his popularity in the Arab world, and it did. His struggle with Iran, coupled with his staunch anti-Israeli policies, made him a hero in the eyes of many Arabs, particularly the Jordanians and Palestinians.

Saddam also sought the support of Western countries that opposed the Iranians. Because the Iranian government was fanatically against any Western influence in the Middle East, the United States and other Western nations supported Iraq in its struggle against Iran. Hoping that Saddam would defeat Iran, the United States, France, and other nations eagerly sold him planes, tanks, and artillery.

In spite of Iraq's military buildup, it did not decisively defeat Iran. In the first months of 1990, Iraq's economy was still reeling from the effects of the war. Many of its oil facilities, destroyed during the war, were still being rebuilt, so some of its vast oil reserves could not be pumped and sold. In addition, Saddam owed a great deal of money to Arab nations that had supported him against Iran. Of Iraq's $80 billion in war debts, half were owed to the Kuwaitis and Saudis.

Why Saddam Wanted Kuwait

Saddam first attempted to raise Iraq's income by increasing the price of oil. Early in 1990, he demanded that all OPEC oil producers raise their prices. But some OPEC members, notably Kuwait, refused to raise their oil prices for fear of losing customers. Without the support of OPEC, Saddam could not raise his oil prices. Saddam became increasingly angry at Kuwait.

Saddam also sought to decrease his war debts. He demanded that Kuwait cancel Iraq's debt of billions of dollars. He said the Kuwaitis should do this out of gratitude to Iraq for stopping the

Saddam Hussein—Knight and Executioner

Saddam Hussein was born in 1937 into a poor Iraqi family. In his teens, he joined the Ba'ath party, which was trying to take control of the Iraqi government. When he was twenty-two, Saddam, whose name means "one who confronts," took part in a machine-gun attack on the car carrying the country's president, Abdul-Karem Kassim. The Ba'athists hoped to eliminate Kassim and seize power. The assassination attempt failed, but the Ba'athists gained power in the 1960s, and Saddam rose quickly through their ranks. One of the party's chief policymakers, he negotiated a treaty with Iran in 1975. The agreement supposedly ended the dispute between the two countries over the Shatt al-Arab waterway. However, soon after ascending to the presidency in 1979, Saddam seized the waterway and attacked Iran. During the bloody war that followed, he approved the use of deadly chemical weapons against the Iranians.

As leader of Iraq in the 1980s, Saddam carried on the Ba'athist policy of harsh dictatorship. American Middle Eastern experts called Saddam's Iraq "one of the most brutal and repressive [strict and controlling] regimes now in power." They noted how Saddam maintained control by exiling people, arresting and detaining them without trials, and torturing and executing them. According to a former Israeli intelligence officer, Saddam is a practical person who "lacks the usual morals common to human beings."

Saddam used his power and money to project a fatherly, heroic image to his people. He ordered that huge paintings and sculptures of himself adorn public squares and buildings. He called himself the modern successor to the kings of Babylon and the "Knight of the Arab Nation," the future leader of the entire Arab world. Many Iraqis began to idolize him. "Saddam, we will give our blood for you!" goes a refrain from an Iraqi children's song. Some Iraqi artists used their own blood to paint his portrait. And Iraqi newspapers declared him to be "the anchor and hope of the meek and the weak." But while Iraqis heaped praises on Saddam, he continued to rule with an iron fist. In the late 1980s, in an attempt to suppress protests, he used chemical weapons on his own people.

Saddam Hussein, president of Iraq since 1979, ordered the invasion of Kuwait in 1990.

After meeting with U.S. president George Bush about the Iraqi invasion that left him in exile, Jaber al-Ahmad al Sabah, emir of Kuwait, delivers parting remarks to the press in Washington, D.C.

Iranians from overrunning Kuwait during the war. The Kuwaitis pointed out that Iran had not tried to overrun Kuwait. They ignored Saddam's demands and insisted that Iraq pay its debts.

Convinced that Kuwait stood in the way of Iraq's prosperity, Saddam began considering invading it. His intentions became clear to some Arab leaders months before the actual invasion. In May 1990, at an Arab conference, Saddam demanded money from the Kuwaitis. They bluntly refused. "If they don't give it to me," he told an Arab diplomat, "I'm going to take it from them."

As he thought about it, Saddam realized that taking over Kuwait would benefit Iraq in a number of ways. First and foremost, it would allow Iraq to control the rich Kuwaiti oil fields. This would not only increase Iraq's wealth, but also give it a stronger voice in setting OPEC oil prices. Kuwait was a tempting prize for other reasons. Controlling Kuwait would erase Iraq's war debt and give Iraq valuable and strategic ports on the Persian Gulf. Saddam also cited historical reasons for taking Kuwait. Iraqi and Kuwaiti tribes had been fighting over land for centuries. When the Kuwaitis gained independence in 1961, Iraq reopened these disputes and laid claim to Kuwait. Iraqi troops threatened to overrun Kuwait, but Britain intervened and protected the Kuwaitis. Many Iraqis bitterly remembered this episode, believing that Kuwait rightfully belonged to Iraq.

From Saddam's point of view, there seemed to be little military risk involved in seizing Kuwait. About the size of the state of New Jersey, Kuwait possessed barely one-twenty-fourth the land area of Iraq. With a population of two million, only one-ninth that of Iraq, and an army consisting of only a few thousand men, Kuwait could not adequately defend itself.

Also, Saddam expected little opposition to a takeover of Kuwait from either Arab or Western countries. Most Arabs disapproved of Kuwait's emir, or royal ruler, Jaber al-Ahmad al Sabah, and his family. It seemed safe to assume that other Arab nations would not come to the aid of Kuwait. Saddam reasoned that Western countries like the United States were mainly interested in defending Israel and would not get involved in a dispute between Arabs. Saddam also recalled that the United States, France, and other Western countries had supplied him with arms to fight Iran. He believed that this made him an ally of the West, and he assumed that U.S. and Western support for his regime would continue even after a takeover of Kuwait.

A Barrage of Insults and Threats

The first stage of Saddam's campaign against Kuwait was a series of verbal attacks. These attacks were made up of exaggerations and outright lies designed to make Kuwait look bad to other Arabs. On July 17, 1990, for example, he publicly threatened the use of force against the Kuwaitis if they did not agree to raise oil

Iraqi foreign minister Tarik Aziz leaves a meeting with U.S. secretary of state James Baker in Geneva, Switzerland, in January 1990.

Kuwait

For a thousand years, the flat deserts of Kuwait were the home of nomadic tribes of Arab herders and fishers called Bedouins. The Bedouins still exist in Kuwait and other areas of the Middle East. In the early 1700s, the Anaiza tribe founded the city of Kuwait, which means "the little fortress" in Arabic, near the shores of the Persian Gulf. A ruling family, the Sabahs, soon came to power. Every leader, or emir, of Kuwait since that time has been a member of the Sabah family. One of the most important emirs, Mubarak al-Sabah, signed a treaty with Britain in 1899 making Kuwait a British protectorate. This meant that Britain handled Kuwait's foreign affairs and protected it against aggression.

When oil was discovered in Kuwait in the 1930s, everyday life began to change. Most Kuwaitis gave up herding, fishing, and pearl diving and became involved in some aspect of oil production. By the 1980s, thanks to oil profits, Kuwait had become one of the world's richest nations. Most Kuwaiti citizens enjoyed comfortable lives supported by generous government benefits and privileges. Abundant wealth allowed many Kuwaitis to hire foreign servants and workers, most of these from Egypt, India, Pakistan, and Iran.

Just one week before Iraq invaded Kuwait, Saddam Hussein assured Egyptian president Hosni Mubarak (above) that he would not invade Kuwait.

prices. Said Saddam, Kuwaiti refusals to do so were part of a "plot" between the Americans and Kuwaitis. Their plan, he charged, was to afford the United States a cheap flow of oil, make the Kuwaitis rich, and hurt other Arab economies. In a speech on Iraqi television, Saddam gave notice to the Kuwaitis: "If words fail to protect Iraqis, something effective must be done to return things to their natural course and return usurped [stolen] rights to their owners.… Iraqis will not forget the maxim [old saying] that cutting necks is better than cutting the means of living. Oh, God Almighty, be witness that we have warned them."

The next day, Iraq's foreign minister Tarik Aziz delivered a letter to the Arab League. The letter charged that Kuwait was involved in a Western-supported Zionist plot designed to depress oil prices and bankrupt other Arab nations in the Middle East. According to Aziz, the Zionists wanted to weaken the Arabs so that the Arabs could no longer threaten Israel. Aziz also claimed that the Kuwaitis had stolen $2.4 billion worth of oil over a period of ten years from an Iraqi oil field near the border between the two countries. One way or another, said Aziz, the Kuwaitis would pay for their treachery. Large numbers of Iraqi troops began to move toward the Kuwaiti border.

Kuwaiti spokesmen emphatically denied the existence of an oil plot and insisted that their country had never stolen oil from anyone. Alarmed at Iraq's warlike stance, the Kuwaiti emir dispatched messengers to the Arab capitals of the region to ask for their assistance if Iraq attacked his country. He also put Kuwait's twenty-thousand-man army on full alert.

By July 23, 1990, more than 100,000 Iraqi soldiers had massed along the Iraqi-Kuwaiti border. Saddam tried to make this troop buildup look innocent by insisting that his army posed no threat to Kuwait. "We don't want war," he told some foreign diplomats in Baghdad. "We hate war. We know what war does." On July 24, Saddam assured Egypt's president Hosni Mubarak that he had no intention of invading Kuwait. The Iraqi leader repeated the same message to the U.S. ambassador to Iraq. Because they took Saddam at his word, most world leaders were surprised and shocked when Iraqi tanks rolled into Kuwait only one week later.

Kuwait Is Overrun

At 2:00 A.M. on August 2, 1990, the powerful Iraqi army launched a sudden and massive attack on Kuwait. Tens of thousands of Iraqi soldiers poured over the border. They quickly overwhelmed a small force of Kuwaiti border guards, Kuwait's only line of defense against invasion. The Iraqi troops were supported by thousands of tanks, armored vehicles, and artillery pieces.

The invaders moved swiftly down the six-lane highway leading to Kuwait City, the country's capital and home to two-thirds of its people. Most Kuwaitis were still asleep, but Kuwaiti lookout stations flashed warnings of the invasion to the royal palace. Kuwaiti leaders attempted to organize a defense of the city, but they had too few troops and too little time.

It was still dark when Iraqi soldiers reached Kuwait City. Small groups of Kuwaiti soldiers and civilians armed with rifles opened fire on the invaders. But the resisters were no match for the Iraqi tanks and armored vehicles that blasted away at buildings, cars, and practically anything that moved. As the Iraqis

(top) A passing motorist took this photograph of Iraqi troops in Kuwait City hours after the August 2, 1990, invasion. (bottom) In Kuwait City, an Iraqi tank and soldier guard the Kuwait Sheraton Hotel, which has been fortified against attack.

neared the palace, the emir loaded his family into a helicopter. He felt that the best thing he could do for his country at that point was seek outside help. Amid the gunfire and explosions of the battle, the helicopter lifted off, banked low over the gulf, and sped southward toward Saudi Arabia. The emir's younger brother elected to stay behind with the palace guards. They all died less than an hour later in a futile defense of the palace.

During the morning and afternoon of August 2, Kuwaiti troops and armed civilians continued as best they could to resist the huge Iraqi war machine. But the Kuwaitis' situation was hopeless. Units of Kuwait's tiny army were scattered around the country and could not be organized into an effective fighting force. Kuwaiti troops had minimal military training and no battle experience. By contrast, the Iraqi troops spearheading the invasion were members of Saddam's Republican Guards. Iraq's best soldiers, they were well trained, and most had seen action in the Iraq-Iran war. The Kuwaitis also faced large portions of Iraq's formidable force of 5,500 tanks. Almost all of Kuwait's 275 tanks had been captured by the Iraqis in the first few hours of the invasion. By the end of the first day, the Iraqis managed to crush Kuwaiti resistance in Kuwait City and other key towns. Iraq's takeover of Kuwait was complete.

The Saudis, shocked and angered at Saddam's attack on fellow Arabs, immediately offered protection to the Kuwaiti emir and his family. The emir ordered the Kuwaiti ambassador to the United Nations to inform the world about Iraq's aggression. He also opened a communications link with the United States and pleaded with American authorities to help his country. Next, the emir delivered a dramatic radio address. He spoke directly to his people, but the speech contained clear warnings to Iraq. "Let them take the chalice [cup] of death," he said. "They have come to kill the sons of Kuwait and its women. We shall fight them everywhere until we clean their treachery from our land.... The entire world is with us!" As world leaders began expressing their outrage over Iraq's actions, it appeared that the emir was not exaggerating.

The World Reacts to the Invasion

Most countries immediately condemned the takeover of Kuwait. U.S. response was especially strong. President George Bush called the Iraqi move "naked aggression" and ordered U.S. economic sanctions, or penalties, against Iraq. His intention was to persuade Saddam to leave Kuwait by hurting the Iraqis financially. First, Bush froze the $20 billion of Iraqi money in U.S. banks, making it impossible for the Iraqis to withdraw or earn interest on their money. Britain and France, whose banks also contained large sums of Iraqi money, did the same. Next, Bush banned all

The USS Independence *was the first aircraft carrier ordered to the Persian Gulf after Iraq invaded Kuwait.*

U.S. imports of Iraqi oil, which constituted approximately 4 percent of total U.S. oil consumption.

President Bush did not stop with economic sanctions. As a warning to the Iraqis to leave Kuwait, Bush ordered the aircraft carrier USS *Independence* into the Persian Gulf. There, it joined eight other U.S. warships that had guarded oil tankers during the Iraq-Iran war. Saddam reacted defiantly to Bush's moves. "We swear," he threatened, "that we will make the Gulf a graveyard for all those who think of committing aggression, starting with these cowardly American navies."

Many other countries joined the United States in calling for Iraq to get out of Kuwait. The United Nations convened an emergency session on the evening of August 2, only hours after the fall of Kuwait. The fifteen-member Security Council, the U.N.'s decision-making branch, passed a resolution to condemn Iraq and demand that it withdraw its troops. Only Yemen, an Arab country sympathetic to Iraq, refused to vote. The council added the warning that U.N.-sponsored economic sanctions might be used if Iraq did not comply. The Soviet Union was among the countries that voted yes to the resolution. Many people found this surprising because the Soviets had sold the Iraqis more weapons than any other country. In addition to voting to condemn the invasion, the Soviets suspended all arms shipments to Iraq, calling for "a swift and unconditional withdrawal of Iraqi forces from Kuwaiti territory."

The next afternoon, the United States and the Soviet Union issued a joint statement, something the two superpowers had never done before. U.S. secretary of state James Baker and Soviet foreign minister Eduard Shevardnadze strongly condemned "the brutal and illegal invasion of Kuwait. Today, we take the unusual step of jointly calling upon the rest of the international community to join with us in an international cutoff of all arms supplies to Iraq." This joint statement was significant. The crisis had given the two superpowers, who normally opposed each other in the Middle East, a common cause in the region. Some diplomats suggested that this might make future problems in the area easier to solve.

What Would Saddam Do Next?

Many world leaders worried that Saddam's aggression might not stop with Kuwait. Saudi leaders privately warned the United States and other Western countries that Saudi Arabia could be Iraq's next target. Although militarily stronger than the Kuwaitis, the Saudis had little chance against Iraq's army, which some experts called the fourth largest in the world. The Saudis and others argued that Saddam was trying to corner the world oil market. Taking Kuwait, they explained, gave him control of 20 percent of the world's oil. With the vast Saudi oil fields, he would control 45 percent. Many Arabs, like Saad Jabr, an Iraqi politician living in exile in London, warned that Saddam should not be trusted. "Knowing Saddam," said Jabr, "if in 30 days nothing happens except verbal threats, he will take over the eastern part of Saudi Arabia [where the oil fields are located].... And if anyone moves against him, he will threaten to blow it up."

U.S. secretary of state James Baker (left) and Soviet foreign minister Eduard Shevardnadze issue a joint statement condemning Iraqi aggression in Kuwait.

With all the talk about a possible Iraqi attack on Saudi Arabia, many Americans worried that President Bush might send U.S. troops to defend the Saudi oil fields. They feared that such a move might increase Middle Eastern tensions and engulf the entire region in a bloody war. Tens of thousands of people, including many Americans, might die.

Fear of such a conflict was not restricted to the United States. Government leaders around the world debated what to do about the invasion. Saddam's aggression had created a dangerous international crisis. This, said some Arab diplomats, was something Saddam had not expected. To save face, or avoid embarrassment, they predicted, he would likely refuse to get out of Kuwait. He might even officially annex the tiny country, making it part of Iraq. The world community would then be left with two painful choices: turn its back and abandon the Kuwaitis or use military force to oust the Iraqis.

CHAPTER THREE

"Desert Shield"–The World Against Iraq

Saddam Hussein had not expected such a huge international outcry against his takeover of Kuwait. His invasion badly hurt his image, especially with countries that had supported him like the United States, the Soviet Union, and France. But, in Saddam's view, immediately leaving Kuwait, as world opinion demanded, would only damage his image further. While his image was now that of an aggressor, backing down might give the world the idea that he was weak and cowardly. This would surely destroy his credibility with Middle Eastern Arabs like the Palestinians. They looked to him as a strong leader, who would stand up against any odds. So, Saddam chose to hold on to Kuwait, gambling that the world community would eventually tire of protesting, and the crisis fade.

But Saddam's stubborn refusal to get out of Kuwait had the opposite effect. In the eyes of most other nations, the takeover of Kuwait set a dangerous precedent. If they allowed Saddam to hold on to his prize, he might attack other countries. And other dictators around the world would get the message that they could attack their neighbors without fear of international police action. The world community had another reason for taking strong action against Saddam. His invasion had placed him in a position to control much of the Middle Eastern oil market. He might later use this power as a weapon to hurt the economies of other nations. Instead of fading, as Saddam had hoped, the crisis intensified for many months as members of the world community took steps to force the Iraqis out of Kuwait.

George Bush—Playing Fair and Dealing with Bullies

Born in 1924 in Milton, Massachusetts, George Herbert Walker Bush enlisted in the U.S. Navy in the early days of World War II. At age eighteen, he was, for a time, the youngest American fighter pilot. During the Pacific conflict, he flew fifty-eight combat missions and was rescued by a submarine after being shot down. After the war, Bush attended Yale University, graduating with a degree in economics in 1948. He then became an executive for a Texas-based oil company.

In 1966, Bush entered politics, winning a Texas seat in the U.S. House of Representatives. President Richard Nixon appointed him U.S. ambassador to the United Nations in 1971. There, among other things, Bush argued for the presence of an international peacekeeping force in the Middle East. Although he supported

Nixon, Bush had the courage to ask him to resign when it became apparent that Nixon had lied during the Watergate scandal. Bush then served as ambassador to China and head of the Central Intelligence Agency, or CIA, under President Ford.

Bush ran for the Republican nomination for president in 1980 but lost to Ronald Reagan. Reagan then asked Bush to become his running mate. In two terms as vice president, Bush traveled to more than sixty countries and headed task forces fighting crime, terrorism, and drug smuggling.

While running for president in 1988, Bush called for the establishment of a "kinder, gentler nation." After winning the election and becoming the nation's forty-first president, he worked to improve relations with the Soviet Union. He also ordered American troops into Panama to depose the dictator Manuel Noriega and restore the government elected by the Panamanian people. Eight months later, Bush found himself facing off with another foreign dictator when Saddam Hussein invaded Kuwait. Many journalists have pointed out that Bush's old-fashioned American upbringing shaped his attitudes about dealing with international criminals and bullies. Commented *Newsweek*'s Evan Thomas, "Bush is a product of a culture that prized not only good breeding and proper manners, but...[also physical strength and moral courage]. As a child, Bush was taught to play fair, but he was also taught to punch a bully in the nose."

George Bush as a young naval officer in 1942. Bush flew fifty-eight missions as a fighter pilot in World War II.

(left) Soldiers leaving for Saudi Arabia struggle to regain their composure after making tearful farewells to loved ones. (right) Members of the Twenty-fourth Infantry Division arrive in Saudi Arabia to take part in Operation Desert Shield.

The United Nations Takes Action

The United Nations Security Council took the first step against Saddam on August 2. The U.N. demanded that the Iraqi leader pull his troops out of Kuwait and threatened to impose economic sanctions on Iraq if he refused. Security Council members then waited four days for him to comply. During that time, Saddam showed no sign of beginning an Iraqi withdrawal. In fact, there were reports that Iraqi soldiers were looting stores and shooting Kuwaiti citizens. Council members felt that there was no choice but to impose the previously threatened sanctions.

On August 6, the council voted on and approved a sweeping trade embargo against Iraq. U.N. Resolution number 661 called for all countries immediately to halt all trade with Iraq and stop any financial and commercial dealings with the Iraqis. This action was dramatic and significant. It marked only the third time in the U.N.'s history that the organization had imposed sanctions on a member country. And the sanctions against Iraq were by far the most severe. The goal was simple: to make the Iraqis leave Kuwait by hurting them financially. Within hours, Iraq felt the first effects of the sanctions as the Turks shut down the pipeline that carried Iraqi oil through Turkey to foreign markets.

The U.N. embargo constituted clear evidence that the international community was willing to take steps against Iraq. This was the support Bush needed to justify sending troops. Many world leaders believed that the sanctions, by themselves, were not enough to prevent an Iraqi takeover of Saudi Arabia. Bush, as well as British, French, Saudi, and other leaders, believed that U.S. troops should be stationed in Saudi Arabia. This would send a clear signal to Saddam that an assault on the Saudis would not be tolerated. The leaders also felt that the sanctions would be more effective if they were accompanied by a show of military force. With world opinion now firmly on his side, Bush decided to act.

U.S. Forces Head for the Middle East

On August 7, 1990, the day the embargo against Iraq took effect, President Bush announced that he was ordering troops to Saudi Arabia. "This will not stand," Bush angrily told the American press. "This will not stand, this aggression against Kuwait." The president acknowledged that sending in the U.S. military was a calculated risk but declared firmly that there was no choice. He said that he intended "to stand up for what's right and condemn what's wrong."

Bush dubbed the defense of Saudi Arabia operation Desert Shield. He immediately mobilized more than 50,000 U.S. troops and ordered that at least 100,000 more prepare to ship out. Within hours, squadrons of F-15 fighter planes and paratroopers from the Eighty-second Airborne Division were on their way to the Middle East. Special radar-equipped planes called AWACs and huge B-52 bombers fueled up and headed toward Saudi Arabia. Joining them were large numbers of deadly F-111 fighter bombers stationed in England and Turkey.

At the same time, the massive aircraft carrier USS *Eisenhower* and its escort warships, stationed in the Mediterranean, went into

(above) A fully armed F-15 fighter jet flies low over the sands of Saudi Arabia during desert maneuvers. (right) F-18 fighters fly in tight formation over the Persian Gulf during Operation Desert Shield.

(left) Marines are drilled on the use of HAWK antiaircraft missiles in preparation for combat. (right) The USS Saratoga *dwarfs a mosque as it passes through the Suez Canal on its way to the Persian Gulf.*

action. They moved quickly through the Suez Canal and into the Red Sea. This placed the carrier's attack planes within striking distance of Iraqi targets. The carrier *Saratoga* and its escorts left Florida, bound for the Persian Gulf. Accompanying them was the battleship *Wisconsin,* carrying cruise missiles. These computer-guided weapons fly only a few hundred feet above ground level and strike with deadly accuracy.

Many countries, including England, France, and Saudi Arabia, publicly praised Bush's show of military force. But some government leaders, including several U.S. congressmen, were worried. They warned that a confrontation between the Americans and Iraqis might provoke Saddam to attack U.S. forces and Israel too. The Middle East might then be engulfed in war. The world marketplace reflected this fear. To cover themselves in case Middle East oil supplies became scarce, oil companies around the world sharply raised their prices. Financial markets such as the New York Stock Exchange were unsure of how a war might affect the value of oil and other commodities. A flurry of panic buying and selling made these markets unstable.

Attempting to ease these fears, President Bush stated that his aim was not to provoke a war. "Four simple principles guide our policy," he explained. "First, we seek the immediate, unconditional, and complete withdrawal of all Iraqi forces from Kuwait. Second, Kuwait's legal government must be restored…. And third, my administration, as has been the case with every president from President Roosevelt to President Reagan, is committed to the security and stability of the Persian Gulf. And fourth, I am determined to protect the lives of American citizens abroad."

The Arab World Split

Saddam Hussein reacted defiantly to President Bush's military buildup in Saudi Arabia. First, Saddam tried to appeal to his many Arab supporters in the Middle East. Attempting to make it appear that U.S. troops were there to harm Arabs, he threatened to "pluck out the eyes of those who attack the Arab nation." On August 8, 1990, Saddam boldly announced that Iraq had formally annexed Kuwait. To justify this action, as well as the invasion, in the eyes of Arabs, he invented a story designed to make it appear that he was helping the Kuwaitis. Saddam claimed that the Kuwaiti people had overthrown their corrupt emir and begged for Iraq to help them. Supposedly, the Kuwaitis wanted to return to the "mother homeland" of Iraq. "Thank God," Saddam said, "that we are now one people, one state that will be the pride of the Arabs." Most members of the world community quickly condemned the annexation of Kuwait. By a vote of 15 to 0, the U.N. Security Council declared the annexation null and void. But most of the Arabs who backed Saddam declared their approval of his actions against Kuwait and vowed to help him against the United States.

But Saddam's supporters represented a minority of Arabs. A large portion of the Arab world was shocked and horrified by Saddam's attack on and annexation of Kuwait. Voicing the opinion of many Arabs, Saudi Arabia's King Fahd called the Iraqi invasion "the most vile aggression known to the Arab nation in its modern history." He tried to reassure Arabs who feared the presence of U.S. troops in the Middle East. U.S. forces, said

(left) Arabs in a Jordanian city march to protest the Western military presence in the Persian Gulf. (right) Iraqi soldiers of the volunteer Popular Army take part in weapons training near Baghdad.

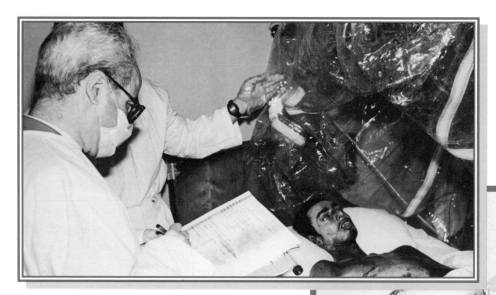

(above) A U.N. doctor attends to a patient suffering from the effects of chemical weapons used by Iraq during the Iraq-Iran war. Western military leaders of Operation Desert Storm feared Iraq would again use chemical weapons in the Persian Gulf War. (right) Egyptian troops wear gas masks during a chemical weapons drill.

the king, "are here to help defend the kingdom [of Saudi Arabia]...and will leave as soon as the kingdom so demands."

Many other Arabs opposed Iraq's policies. The Egyptians resented Saddam even before the invasion of Kuwait. Before Iraq's 1980s military buildup, Egypt had been the strongest, most influential country in the Middle East. Arabs had looked upon Egypt's capital of Cairo as the region's most important city. Egyptians were offended by Saddam's attempts to make Baghdad the political center of the Middle East. Immediately after Iraq annexed Kuwait on August 8, Egypt's president Mubarak ordered Egyptian troops to Saudi Arabia to back up the Americans. "If anyone starts attacking," warned Mubarak, "we are ready to confront him." This marked the first time in history that Arabs had joined with outsiders to confront other Arabs. Syria also sent troops to help the Saudis, as did Morocco, a North African Arab nation.

These countries criticized Saddam at an August 10 emergency meeting of the Arab League in Cairo. The Iraqi dictator countered them with a bitter verbal attack that shocked many Arabs. Sending a message from his palace in Baghdad, Saddam called upon all Arabs and Moslems to begin a jihad against all foreign troops and "corrupt" Arab rulers. He tried to incite the jihad by falsely claiming that the Americans and Zionists had captured the holy city of Mecca. He called upon his followers to "burn the land under the feet of the aggressive invaders."

Egyptian, Syrian, Saudi, and other Arab leaders swiftly rejected Saddam's words, calling them warlike and misguided. Delegates from Egypt and other moderate Arab states drafted a resolution denouncing the annexation of Kuwait. The resolution also endorsed U.N. sanctions against Iraq and called for the creation of an Arab military force to keep the peace. Of the twenty-one members of the league, twelve voted in favor of the resolution. Of the remaining members, Iraq, Libya, and the PLO voted no, and the other six refused to vote. Thus, although the Arab League made an official stand against Iraq, the voting indicated that a sizable minority of Arabs still backed Saddam.

Saddam Threatens His Enemies

After the Arab League's vote, Saddam announced that Iraq would never leave Kuwait unless the Israelis withdrew from the territories they had occupied in the 1967 and 1973 wars. Western and Arab officials saw this as Saddam's attempt to bolster his image with the Arab masses, who bitterly resent Israel. Apparently, Saddam believed that linking his takeover of Kuwait with the Israeli issue would win him the support of most Arabs. But moderate Arabs, like the Egyptians and Saudis, as well as the Western nations, rejected this idea, insisting that the two

Air Force sergeant Robb Perk explains the correct use of a gas mask to members of the press assigned to cover the war in the Persian Gulf.

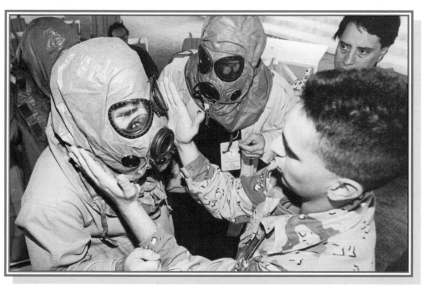

Chemical Weapons

As the likelihood of war in the Middle East increased in the last months of 1990, Americans and their allies worried about Iraq's arsenal of chemical weapons.

After the World War I gas attacks, world leaders held the view that using poison gases on people was unusually cruel and inhumane. So they outlawed the use of chemical weapons in the 1925 Geneva Protocol. However, this treaty did not prohibit nations from producing and stockpiling such weapons.

In the 1980s, Western intelligence reports indicated that the Iraqis had amassed between two thousand and four thousand tons of chemical weapons. In an attempt both to cripple and terrorize the enemy, Saddam used poison gas against the Iranians in the Iraq-Iran war. He also unleashed chemical weapons on the Kurds, Iraq's largest ethnic group, in northern Iraq to suppress Kurdish protests and rebellions. In the fall of 1990, some Iraqi diplomats warned that Saddam would not hesitate to use the same weapons on Americans or other "foreign invaders" who posed a threat to Iraq. Preparing for the worst, U.S. commanders began supplying gas masks and special protective suits to all U.S. troops and personnel heading for the Middle East.

The Threat of Terrorism

Saddam Hussein's large army and stockpiles of chemical weapons were not the only threats posed to U.S. and Allied forces moving into Saudi Arabia. Saddam also made it clear that if he was attacked, his supporters would open a "second front" against Western military and civilian targets. He was referring to organized acts of terrorism such as bombings and airplane hijackings. Terrorism is violence committed to force others to submit to one's personal or political demands. In September and October 1990, known terrorists such as Abul Abbas and Abu Nidal set up headquarters in Baghdad. These international criminals enjoyed the support and cooperation of Iraqi authorities. Abbas warned that if American forces fired on the Iraqis, "We will adopt any method. The world is wide open to us."

U.S. leaders feared that Arab terrorists might try to attack American military installations as they did in Lebanon in 1983. In that year, a truck carrying explosives slammed into a U.S. barracks, killing 241 American soldiers. To discourage a similar attack in Saudi Arabia, specially trained commandos guarded U.S. and Allied military leaders. Extra guards were assigned to protect Gen. Norman Schwarzkopf, the commander of operation Desert Shield. The commandos spoke fluent Arabic to help them detect Arab terrorists trying to sneak through the American lines.

Many Westerners also feared attacks on Americans aboard foreign airplane flights and at European and Middle Eastern airports. As a result, many tourists and businesspeople cancelled foreign trips in the fall and winter of 1990. In an effort to prevent terrorist incidents, airports, embassies, banks, and police organizations around the world increased security measures.

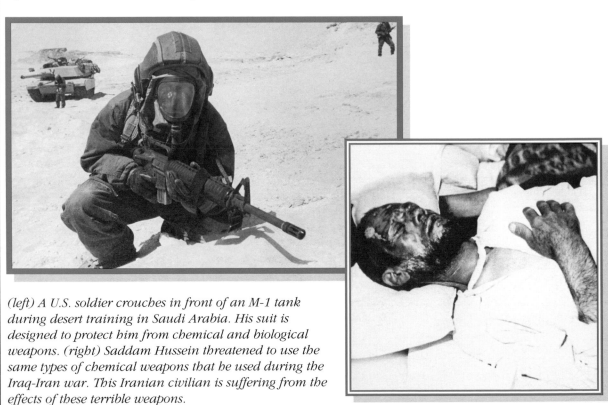

(left) A U.S. soldier crouches in front of an M-1 tank during desert training in Saudi Arabia. His suit is designed to protect him from chemical and biological weapons. (right) Saddam Hussein threatened to use the same types of chemical weapons that he used during the Iraq-Iran war. This Iranian civilian is suffering from the effects of these terrible weapons.

issues were separate. They called Saddam's proposal a "desperate move" that served only to inflame the crisis initiated by Iraq.

Angered by international condemnation, Saddam and other Iraqi officials threatened to destroy any armies, Arab or otherwise, that dared to interfere in Iraq's business. Other warnings from Baghdad followed, some directed specifically at the Americans and other Westerners. One issue that concerned world leaders was that Iraqi spokesmen refused to rule out Iraq's use of chemical weapons if attacked. Western leaders did not take this threat lightly. They recalled that Saddam had used poison gas on the Iranians in the 1980s in violation of international laws against the use of such weapons.

Saddam also warned that his Moslem supporters would help Iraq by striking at its enemies around the world. This was a reference to terrorist groups that had committed acts of violence against the West before. One worried U.S. official predicted, "If we push this guy [Saddam] too hard, bombs will go off in Europe." A week after the invasion of Kuwait, the U.S. State Department issued a warning to Americans about "the risk of terrorist incidents directed against American interests overseas."

Another ominous Iraqi threat concerned the fate of foreigners living in or visiting Iraq and Kuwait. These included approximately thirty-five hundred Americans, five thousand British, and several thousand citizens of France, the Soviet Union, and other countries. One of Saddam's ministers warned, "Countries that resort to…[war against] Iraq should remember they have interests and nationals [citizens] in Kuwait." In the United States, State Department phones were jammed with calls from worried relatives of Americans in the Middle East. U.S. diplomats worked day and night trying to make contact with Americans still in Kuwait.

The Crisis Intensifies

On August 17, 1990, the Iraqis acted on their threat against the foreign nationals. U.S., British, and other foreign citizens were not allowed to leave Iraq or Kuwait. An Iraqi spokesman said that the nationals would stay "as long as Iraq remains threatened with an aggressive war." Saddam said that he would free the foreigners if the United States got out of Saudi Arabia. Three days later, Saddam announced that Iraq had begun moving Westerners to key military and industrial sites. This, he said, was to discourage the United States from bombing Iraqi targets. This use of hostages as "human shields" against attack outraged most nations. The United States, Britain, and the other affected countries issued strong protests, saying that taking hostages was a violation of international law. Iraq responded by insisting that the foreigners were not hostages, but only "guests." Said an angry President Bush, "When Saddam Hussein specifically offers to trade the freedom of those citizens of many nations he holds against their will in return for concessions [meeting his demands], there can be little doubt that whatever these innocent people are called, they are in fact hostages."

Saddam also ordered all foreign embassies in Kuwait to shut down. Representatives of the United States, Britain, France, the Soviet Union, Germany, Italy, Spain, Denmark, Sweden, and Finland immediately called this demand "unacceptable." All refused to close their embassies because they did not recognize the Iraqi takeover of Kuwait as legal.

Saddam Hussein's takeover of Kuwait had now become an international crisis affecting countries from every part of the globe. All nations were forbidden to conduct trade with the Iraqis, who had taken hostages openly and threatened terrorism against those who opposed Saddam. As the Middle East moved toward the brink of war, most government leaders were unsure what the Iraqi dictator might do next. Some U.S. officials remarked that, with the world against him, Saddam's defiant and threatening stance seemed stupid and senseless. They were not reassured when Iraq's foreign minister, Tarik Aziz, aimed a threat directly at President Bush on August 21. Warned Aziz, "If the American leader thinks that this is a vacation like they had in Panama and Grenada [two small countries occupied by U.S. troops], they are mistaken....It will be a bloody conflict, and America will lose and...be humiliated."

CHAPTER FOUR

"We Won't Pull Any Punches"–Prelude to War

By the beginning of September 1990, most nations had condemned Iraq's takeover of Kuwait. The U.N.'s economic sanctions against Iraq were in effect, and huge numbers of Allied troops continued to pour into Saudi Arabia. Yet Saddam Hussein still refused to pull Iraqi troops out of Kuwait. He even showed contempt for world opinion by announcing that he had made Kuwait the nineteenth province of Iraq.

Since it seemed increasingly unlikely that Iraq would give up Kuwait, President George Bush considered using military force. Bush realized that such a large-scale operation would require the support of the American public. Would the American people feel that there was sufficient cause to commit U.S. troops to the Middle East?

Justifying War Against Iraq

Bush and many of his advisors felt that there were several factors that justified U.S. military action against Iraq. First, there was intense concern in the United States for the safety of the Kuwaiti people. According to reports trickling out of Kuwait, the Iraqi occupation was brutal and inhumane. There were confirmed reports of atrocities, acts of unusual violence and cruelty, committed by Iraqi soldiers. People who had managed to escape from Kuwait said they had witnessed Iraqis raping and murdering Kuwaitis, as well as looting and destroying Kuwaiti property. These reports created a feeling of urgency in the United States, as well as in the international community as a whole. Many Americans

Iraq and the Atomic Bomb

As tensions in the Middle East increased during the winter of 1990, many world leaders voiced their concerns that Saddam Hussein was in the process of developing nuclear weapons. Many Western scientists claimed that there was nothing to worry about yet. Although Iraq had a nuclear program, they said, Iraqi scientists were still several years away from actually constructing a working atomic bomb. But President Bush was less optimistic. "Every day that passes," he warned, "brings Saddam one step closer to realizing his goal of a nuclear weapons arsenal."

Bush's supporters believed the Iraqis had amassed about three hundred tons of the uranium compounds needed to build atomic bombs. Early in 1990, British agents broke up an Iraqi smuggling ring that tried to sneak Western nuclear trigger devices into Iraq. Bush insisted that, sooner or later, the Iraqi nuclear program would become a serious threat to peace in the Middle East. Said Bush, "No one knows precisely when this dictator [Saddam] may acquire atomic weapons. But we do know this for sure: He has never possessed a weapon that he didn't use."

expressed the view that war with Iraq was the only way to save Kuwait from total destruction.

Another factor that weighed in favor of using force against Iraq was the failure of the U.N. embargo. Iraq's loss of trade was costing it millions of dollars per day. Yet the country showed no signs of giving in to this pressure. Even if the embargo worked, some people argued, it might take years. By that time, Iraq would have completely destroyed Kuwait.

In addition, Iraq possessed large stores of chemical weapons and possibly biological, or germ, weapons. These could unleash deadly diseases like bubonic plague on Iraq's enemies. There was also evidence that the Iraqis were trying desperately to build nuclear weapons. The Iraqis already owned Soviet-made missiles that could carry these weapons to other parts of the Middle East, including Israel. Bush and many others in the United States worried that, once in possession of nuclear weapons, Iraq would be a threat to the entire Middle East. There seemed little doubt in the minds of most Americans that Saddam Hussein would not hesitate to use such weapons. His brutal takeover of Kuwait and subsequent seizure of thousands of hostages seemed to confirm that he was a ruthless, dangerous man. Thus, Bush felt that a war against Iraq at that time might deter a larger, more destructive war later.

American Concerns

All these reasons seemed to indicate that the American public would support U.S. intervention in Iraq. But there were also serious concerns about U.S. military involvement. One of these concerns was the role Israel might play in a U.S. war with Iraq. The United States still strongly supported Israel, and many Americans worried that if the United States attacked Iraq, Saddam might retaliate by attacking Israel. If this were to happen, Israel might retaliate immediately. If Israel attacked Iraq, the Saudis and other moderate Arabs, still strongly anti-Israel, might then turn on the United States and its Western allies. The United States would then be faced with a difficult choice: either pull out of the Middle East and abandon Kuwait or join with the Israelis against all Arabs. A war with all Arab nations would have been completely unacceptable to most Americans, and they would have opposed it. They would also have eventually opposed a continuing U.S.-Iraqi conflict that dragged on for months or years.

Americans were also concerned about U.S. soldiers. Military action against Iraq would require large numbers of U.S. troops, more than the small regular army could supply. Thousands of reservists would have to be called up. These are civilians who spend a few weeks each year in military training. Some people worried that there would not be enough time to train the

reservists properly for a grueling war in the deserts. Iraqi soldiers, used to fighting in that region, might have the advantage. Hundreds of American soldiers might die. The sight of Americans coming home in body bags over a foreign war could also turn Americans against continuing U.S. intervention. There was also the emotional issue of women serving in both the regular army and in the reserves. In 1990, more than 11 percent of U.S. forces were women, the highest proportion in the country's history. Many Americans feared that even though they were not allowed in combat, hundreds or thousands of American women might be killed by Iraqi missiles or bombs.

(left) After arriving in Saudi Arabia, nineteen-year-old Lori Leininger (right) of the U.S. Army's Eighteenth Airborne Division prepares for a drill with fellow soldiers. (right) Iraqi reservists train for war in the Persian Gulf. Western military leaders feared Iraqi soldiers would be better trained for desert combat than American soldiers.

The United States Gears Up for War

As President Bush and other American leaders weighed the pros and cons of war with Iraq, they continued to increase U.S. troop and equipment levels in Saudi Arabia. U.S. armed forces, military bases, factories, and transportation networks mobilized in the largest American military buildup since the Vietnam War. On August 22, 1990, one American official commented that the United States had moved the equivalent of a midwestern town the size of Fayette, Indiana, to the Persian Gulf in the space of only two weeks. This included one billion pounds of arms, ammunition, food, household goods, and water. Dozens of cargo ships and planes worked around the clock, carrying troops and supplies from American bases to the Middle East. As the buildup continued, the carrier *John F. Kennedy* and several other warships headed for the gulf.

Several other countries increased their military presence in Saudi Arabia during the following two weeks as well. France raised the number of its troops to thirteen thousand and also

Weapons of the War—the Apache Helicopter

The AH-64 Apache helicopter is one of the U.S. Army's main high-tech antitank weapons. The Apache is also designed to provide air support for ground troops. When the troops approach an enemy position, the Apache flies in front of them. The pilot spots the exact positions of enemy soldiers and then fires on them while the attacking troops move in for the kill. Looking something like a giant wasp, the Apache is capable of climbing 3,240 feet per minute and cruises parallel to the ground at 184 miles per hour.

The Apache is equipped with some of the most advanced computer and laser systems available. Among these is an infrared night-vision system allowing the pilot to fly safely at night at low altitudes. This device picks up infrared rays, which are invisible to the naked eye. Since people, vehicles, trees, the ground, and other materials give off infrared rays, the device renders these objects clearly visible at night.

The Apache also has a radar-warning device that tells the pilot when enemy radar has locked onto the copter. This allows the craft immediately to use evasive maneuvers and escape attack by bullets or missiles. The craft's targeting system magnifies the image of a target miles away in both daytime and nighttime. With nearly pinpoint accuracy, laser beams home in, enabling the pilot to lock onto the target. He or she can choose among such weapons as rapid-firing machine guns, deadly rockets, and powerful antitank missiles with a range of up to five miles.

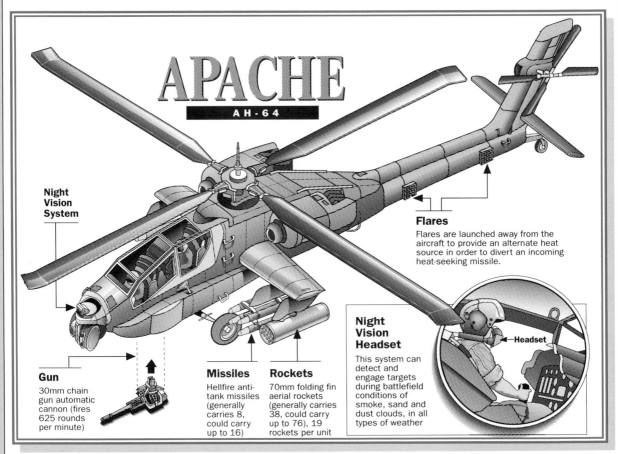

APACHE
AH-64

Night Vision System

Flares
Flares are launched away from the aircraft to provide an alternate heat source in order to divert an incoming heat-seeking missile.

Gun
30mm chain gun automatic cannon (fires 625 rounds per minute)

Missiles
Hellfire anti-tank missiles (generally carries 8, could carry up to 16)

Rockets
70mm folding fin aerial rockets (generally carries 38, could carry up to 76), 19 rockets per unit

Night Vision Headset
This system can detect and engage targets during battlefield conditions of smoke, sand and dust clouds, in all types of weather

←Headset

sent fourteen warships and one hundred antitank helicopters. Britain sent eight thousand troops and 120 tanks. In addition, Secretary of State James Baker and other U.S. and British diplomats convinced many nations to join the growing coalition against Iraq. Italy, Argentina, and Canada joined, sending troops, ships, and warplanes. By mid-September, twenty-two nations had joined the coalition of Allies against Iraq. This buildup of international forces in the Middle East appeared to have little effect on Saddam Hussein. Except for the freeing of about twenty-nine hundred hostages in September 1990, there was no change in the Iraqi position.

Publicly, President Bush expressed the optimistic view that the coalition's massive display of force would eventually make Saddam back down. But privately, Bush and his advisors were convinced that war with Iraq was inevitable. They met secretly in October and planned an invasion of Iraq and Kuwait, which would tentatively begin in January 1991. Bush's top military advisors informed him that many more troops and arms would be

(top) A soldier scurries out of the way of these French Gazelle attack helicopters arriving in Arabia to join the Allied forces there. (bottom) Two self-propelled 155mm howitzers are unloaded from a U.S. Navy cargo ship at a Saudi Arabian port during Operation Desert Shield.

Gen. Colin Powell

Colin Powell, chairman of the joint chiefs, the nation's top-ranking general, is the son of immigrants from the Caribbean island of Jamaica. He grew up in New York's Harlem district. Everybody in his neighborhood, he says, was a member of some minority. "I never thought there was something wrong with me because I'm black," explained Powell. "So when people say to me, 'Weren't you held back?'... my simple answer is, 'My color is somebody else's problem and not mine. You just take me as I am.'" Powell believes that America is a place where any person can achieve success through hard work, and he has proved it. He earned "A's" in college, then entered the army, where he rose quickly through the ranks.

After serving in Vietnam, receiving eleven medals and commanding dozens of military actions, Powell became chairman of the joint chiefs in 1989. Some politicians have called him the "black Eisenhower," comparing him to the general who led U.S. and Allied forces in World War II. Like Eisenhower, they say, Powell was born into poverty, rose through the ranks by hard work, and inspires unswerving loyalty in his troops.

needed for such an operation, and these would take months to transport to the Middle East. So, on November 8, 1990, Bush ordered a huge increase in U.S. troop levels in Saudi Arabia. By early 1991, he said, there would be more than 400,000 American soldiers, as well as thousands of American tanks, ships, and fighter planes involved in operation Desert Shield. This mobilization of U.S. forces, including the call-up of many reserve units, was the largest since World War II.

The Allies Give Iraq a Final Warning

In preparing U.S. forces for war against Iraq, President Bush realized that the United States could not attack without U.N. approval. After all, the United States and other allies were in Saudi Arabia with the permission of the United Nations. Therefore, any military action taken against Iraq would have to have the consent of the majority of U.N. nations. Although Bush was already convinced that force was necessary, he needed to convince the U.N. and other allies.

Early in November 1990, Bush sent James Baker on an eight-day tour of Europe, Asia, and the Middle East. Baker's mission was to gain support for the use of force against Iraq. Meeting with the Kuwaiti emir, the British, Chinese, Soviets, Egyptians, Turks, and many others, Baker argued that the sanctions were working slowly and might not persuade the Iraqis to leave Kuwait. He convinced all the Allies that they should issue Iraq an ultimatum: get out of Kuwait by a given date or risk attack by the Allies. On November 7, British prime minister Margaret

Soldiers charge a fortified position during a combat exercise.

U.S. secretary of state James Baker shakes hands with Iraqi foreign minister Tarik Aziz as they begin negotiations in Geneva, Switzerland, in an attempt to prevent military action in the Persian Gulf.

Thatcher summed up the feelings of most Allied leaders. "Time is running out for Saddam Hussein," she said sternly. "Either he gets out of Kuwait soon or we and our allies will remove him by force and he will go down to defeat with all its consequences. He has been warned."

Baker also took his argument for the use of force to the U.N. Security Council. During the debate that followed, the Kuwaiti ambassador delivered an impassioned plea for the U.N. to approve the use of force. He called upon the members of the council to save his country from "the atrocities of an Iraqi regime which has run amok." On November 29, the Security Council voted to approve U.N. Resolution number 678. The resolution authorized the Allies to use military action against Iraq if it had not pulled out of Kuwait by midnight on January 15, 1991. The vote was 13 to 2, with Yemen and Cuba casting the negative ballots.

The U.N. vote was a major diplomatic victory for Bush, Baker, and other Allied leaders. It marked only the second time in history that the United Nations had approved the use of force against a country. The first time was at the beginning of the Korean War in 1950, when the U.N. sponsored military action against the North Koreans.

Last-Minute Attempts to Avoid War

Pleased with the U.N.'s authorization of the use of force against Iraq, President Bush lashed out at Saddam. Bush called the Iraqi

James Baker

James Addison Baker was born in Houston, Texas, in 1930. After serving in the U.S. Marines, Baker earned a law degree from the University of Texas. His work as an attorney for large corporations gave him valuable experience in negotiating deals that he would use later in politics.

Baker entered the political arena in 1970, when he began managing the political campaigns of his friend George Bush. Later, Baker managed the presidential campaigns of Gerald Ford and Ronald Reagan. President Reagan appointed Baker chief of staff in 1980. In this job, Baker earned a reputation for his abilities to organize and make shrewd political decisions.

Despite Baker's lack of experience in foreign affairs, President Bush assigned Baker the job of secretary of state in 1989. Baker immediately showed his skills as a negotiator. In a series of meetings with Soviet, German, Japanese, and other diplomats, he reached agreements on issues such as trade and arms control. In dealing with foreign heads of state, Baker is known to be patient and understanding, yet also firm and persistent. In the fall of 1990, he almost single-handedly convinced the leaders of more than twenty nations to join the Allied coalition against Iraq.

Spending Christmas in the Desert

After spending Thanksgiving in the Saudi deserts, American soldiers hoped that the crisis would end in time for them to enjoy Christmas at home. But by December 1, 1990, continued tensions in the Middle East had caused this hope to fade. Most GIs tried to make the best of the situation. Pointing at the vast stretches of light brown sand, Cpl. Christopher Williams joked, "At least we'll have a white Christmas."

At first, it appeared that the Saudis would allow no holiday celebrations. Saudi Arabia is a strict Moslem country where all other religions are banned by law. Saudi officials warned that Christmas trees and religious cards would not be permitted. But so many plastic trees and Christmas cards arrived from the United States that Saudi censors gave in. "Just make sure any celebrations are kept quiet and discreet," a Saudi told American commanders.

When a U.S. congressman visited the troops, he asked several GIs what they wanted for Christmas. Some said they wanted a six-pack of beer, since the Saudis also banned the drinking of alcohol. Army MP Kim Thompson's reply echoed what most of America's desert warriors wanted for Christmas 1990—"a date when we're leaving."

leader "a classic bully who thinks he can get away with kicking sand in the face of the world." Bush promised that if force became necessary, "we [the Allies] won't pull any punches." He told the American people that any U.S. action, unlike the fighting in Vietnam, would be swift, massive, and decisive. But Bush was also careful not to give the impression that he actually wanted a war. On November 30, he offered to send Baker on a peace mission to Baghdad in an effort "to go the extra mile for peace." Iraq's Tarik Aziz could then visit Bush in the United States. After some haggling over locations and dates, U.N. negotiators set up a January 9, 1991, meeting in Geneva, Switzerland, between Baker and Aziz.

As the January meeting in Geneva drew closer, tensions around the world increased. Many hoped that Saddam would use the occasion to strike a deal with the Americans and avoid a disastrous war. Allied military commanders were less optimistic. They feared that Saddam might launch a surprise attack prior to January 15 in an attempt to cripple Allied forces before they were completely prepared. Allied troops remained on constant alert in case the Iraqi dictator decided to strike.

On January 9, the eyes of the world were trained on Geneva. The meeting lasted several hours, raising hopes that Baker and Aziz had achieved a settlement. But these hopes were dashed when the meeting ended in a stalemate. According to Baker, Aziz continued to insist that Iraq would not leave Kuwait until the Israelis gave back the lands taken in the Arab-Israeli wars. Baker said he "heard nothing that suggested to me any Iraqi flexibility whatsoever... The choice is Iraq's." Baker warned, "If it should choose to continue its brutal occupation of Kuwait, Iraq will be choosing a military confrontation which it cannot win and which will have devastating consequences for Iraq." Aziz countered that the United States did not really want peace. He told Baker that Arabs would refuse to fight Arabs. In the final moment, he said, the Arab members of the Allied forces would abandon the United States. The Americans would then be left stranded in the desert, where the Iraqis, used to fighting in the sands, would easily defeat them. Aziz also promised that Iraq would attack Israel if the Allies attacked Iraq.

With the failure of the Geneva talks, war between Iraq and the Allies seemed inevitable. But President Bush faced one last obstacle before he could commit U.S. troops to combat. The U.S. Congress had not yet approved the use of force by American soldiers. Beginning on January 8, there was a dramatic four-day congressional debate in which Bush's opponents argued that the sanctions should be given more time. They feared another long war like Vietnam with many U.S. casualties. Asked Senate majority leader George Mitchell, "How many young Americans will die?... And the truly haunting question will be: did they die unnecessarily? For if we go to war now, no one will ever know if the sanctions would have worked."

But Mitchell and those who agreed with him were in the minority. Most lawmakers, like a majority of American citizens, felt that all reasonable efforts for peace had been made. The threat of military force, they believed, was the only effective option left. Senator Joseph Lieberman of Connecticut summed up this viewpoint, saying, "Our final, best chance for a truly peaceful end to this crisis...is to send a clear...message to Saddam Hussein that the American Congress and the American people stand shoulder to shoulder with our president in this critical moment of confrontation." This attitude carried the day. On January 12, Congress voted to approve the use of force if Iraq had not left Kuwait by the U.N. deadline.

In the final three days before the deadline, both the president of France and the U.N. secretary general tried to reason with Saddam. But they failed to convince him that a war against the Allies would be disastrous for Iraq. "Should the Americans become embroiled [involved]," Saddam boasted, "we will make them swim in their own blood, Allah willing." President Bush responded by telling some congressional leaders, "If we get into an armed situation, [Saddam] is going to get his ass kicked." This last-minute bout of verbal sparring by the two leaders left millions around the world with the feeling that there was no way war could be avoided. "Now," remarked an American reporter, "the world holds its breath and asks: when the clock chimes twelve, who will strike first?"

CHAPTER FIVE

"Desert Storm"—The Massive Allied Air Assault

Soldiers from the 101st Airborne Division carry the U.S. flag as they head for a live-ammunition war exercise in the Saudi Arabian desert.

As the last minutes before the January 15, 1991, U.N. deadline ticked away, both Iraqi and Allied forces stood ready. Tens of thousands of Iraqi troops peered from trenches and concrete bunkers constructed in the desert along the Kuwaiti-Saudi border. Tense and worried, they wondered whether the Allies would attack exactly at midnight or prolong the agony by waiting. At the huge Allied air base at Dhahran, on the gulf coast about two hundred miles south of Kuwait, radar operators kept a watchful eye on their screens. They knew that an attack by Iraqi planes or missiles could come at any moment. Allied pilots stood by in their flight suits, awaiting the order to board their planes.

In Israel, pilots sat in the cockpits of their jets twenty-four hours a day. If the signal came, they could be airborne in seconds and on their way to bomb Iraqi targets. Although Israel was not a member of the Allied coalition, Israeli leaders took Saddam's threat to attack Israel very seriously. President Bush had asked the Israelis to show restraint if attacked, but Israeli leaders had not assured him that they would do so. They insisted that any decision about retaliation would have to be made when and if the Iraqis attacked them.

In the United States and other countries, many people could not sleep. Millions sat before their televisions, waiting for the expected news bulletin announcing the beginning of hostilities. Midnight came, but the bulletin did not. To the surprise of many, the deadline passed uneventfully. The morning and afternoon of January 16 dragged on, and still there was no news of fighting in

CNN Scoops the Networks

For decades, the three major American television networks, ABC, CBS, and NBC, had dominated the reporting of U.S. and world news events. But that situation changed dramatically on the evening of January 16, 1991, when U.S. warplanes began their massive assault on Iraq. CNN, the Cable News Network, which broadcasts news twenty-four hours a day, gathered a majority of the huge American viewing audience. As U.S. planes bombed Baghdad, CNN reporters Bernard Shaw, John Holliman, and Peter Arnett provided electrifying live reports from an Iraqi hotel room. They were the only newspeople who managed to continue broadcasting after the bombing began. As a result, CNN won exclusive coverage of the story from the other networks.

In the following days and weeks, CNN continued to lead in war coverage. Its later coverage of the war was not only continuous, but also more complete and in-depth than that of the other networks. CNN reporters provided up-to-the-minute information and video footage to hundreds of independent radio and TV stations. TV news experts say that CNN's rise in popularity was bound to happen sooner or later. As the three major networks continue to close down branches because of economic problems, CNN is opening new bureaus all around the world. It is currently the only news organization in the world that reaches and reports from one hundred nations.

Although some newspeople humorously refer to January 16 as "the night the networks died," ABC, CBS, and NBC also provided coverage of the war. Often broadcasting live, the four networks brought many of the incidents of the conflict directly into people's homes. Never before had ordinary citizens been able to watch the dramatic, startling, and upsetting events of a war unfold before their eyes.

Cable News Network's Peter Arnett continued to report live from Baghdad even after Allied bombing of the city commenced.

Three Americans show concern as they read a news bulletin about the outbreak of fighting in the Persian Gulf.

the Middle East. Some people breathed a sigh of relief. Perhaps, they thought, there would be no war after all. A few theorized that President Bush and other Allied leaders had been bluffing about using force. And Saddam had called their bluff.

But it soon became clear that the Allies were not bluffing. At a few minutes past 7:00 in the evening of January 16, the bulletin that most people had been dreading finally came. President Bush's spokesman Marlin Fitzwater announced to the press that Allied planes had begun bombing Iraqi targets at 4:50 that afternoon. The operation had been dubbed Desert Storm. Said Fitzwater, "The liberation of Kuwait has begun."

Blinding the Iraqi Defenses

Desert Storm was the largest air assault in history. Its goal was to make it impossible for Iraq to attack Saudi Arabia and also weaken the Iraqi army in preparation for a later Allied ground assault to liberate Kuwait. Allied planes were on a mission to destroy Iraqi airfields, missile sites, troop bunkers, army bases, weapons factories, and industrial facilities. The Allies would also strike communications and transportation networks in order to confuse and disrupt Iraqi defensive efforts. At the same time, the planes would bomb as many of Iraq's chemical, biological, and nuclear facilities as possible. Iraq would then be unable to threaten its neighbors with these weapons of mass destruction. The locations of all Iraqi targets had been pinpointed and mapped by special cameras aboard U.S. satellites and high-flying spy planes.

Weapons of the War—Antiradar Weapons

Since its invention in World War II, radar has been an effective way to detect incoming enemy aircraft. A radar antenna sends out invisible radar beams that bounce off the planes and return to a receiver. A radar operator sees the images of the planes on a screen.

At the outset of the Gulf War, the Iraqis had an extensive network of radar facilities. This network allowed them to detect enemy planes entering Iraqi territory. But the Iraqis were totally unprepared for the array of sophisticated antiradar weapons possessed by the Allies. First, the United States unleased its Stealth bombers, which are nearly invisible to radar. Unusual wing and body designs and new materials coating the planes' surfaces deflect or absorb radar beams. This enables the bombers to reach their targets without being detected and shot down.

The Allies also used U.S.-made Electronic CounterMeasures devices, or ECMs. Attached to the U.S. Navy's EA-6B jets, the ECMs detect enemy radar beams and use computers to identify their exact makeup. In a split second, the computer sends out a beam of "white noise," a type of static that jams and blinds the enemy's radar. A lead plane carrying an ECM creates a safe corridor through which other bombers follow, unseen by the enemy, all the way to the target.

The U.S.-made High-Speed Anti-Radiation Missiles, or HARMS, are high-tech devices that destroy enemy radar installations. Fired from F-4G Wild Weasel jets, the HARM missiles home in on the radar beams themselves, reaching and annihilating the antennas. These and other Allied antiradar weapons rendered Iraq's air defenses nearly useless on the first day of the Allied air offensive.

An F-117 Stealth fighter awaits maintenance outside a secret airbase in Saudi Arabia. (below left) A diagram shows how the Stealth bomber's shape helps it elude enemy radar. (below right) ECMs detect enemy radar and send out "white noise" to jam it.

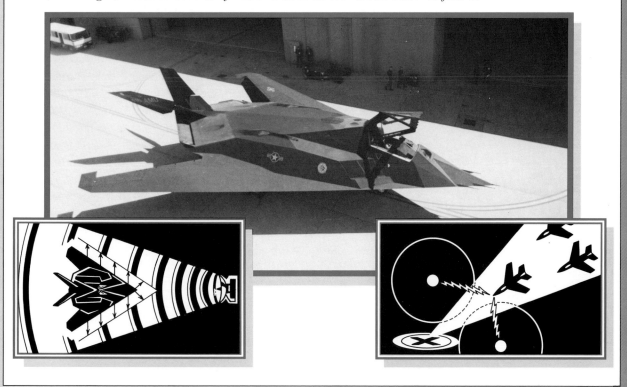

Two A-7E fighters from the aircraft carrier USS John F. Kennedy *make a low-level run over the Arabian desert during Operation Desert Shield. After Desert Shield, the A-7 jets would be replaced by the F-18 jets.*

Hundreds of Allied planes roared off runways in Saudi Arabia and from the decks of carriers in the Red Sea and Persian Gulf. As they converged on Iraq and occupied Kuwait, the first step of the air assault—the elimination of Iraqi radar defenses—began. This was essential to the success of the Allied plan. Radar devices on the ground and in Iraqi aircraft would be able to detect the positions of Allied planes. This would make it easier for Iraqi anti-aircraft guns and missiles to shoot down the invading planes.

Allied jets carrying sophisticated antiradar equipment led the way into Iraqi territory. In the first twenty minutes of the attack, these planes jammed Iraqi radar signals, creating static on radar screens. Meanwhile, other high-tech jets fired missiles that homed in on and obliterated Iraqi radar installations. In less than an hour, all of Iraq's ground radar stations and most Iraqi warplanes were radar "blind." This rendered the Iraqis incapable of detecting or defending against the huge, lethal Allied air armada. A few Iraqi pilots made visual contact with Allied planes and tried to fight. But these Iraqi planes were shot down immediately, and minutes later the rest of Saddam's air force fled northward.

Air Strikes Hammer Iraq

With most of Iraq's radar warning system crippled and the Iraqi air force on the run, Allied bombers and attack planes were free to attack their targets without fear of being shot down. American F-117A Stealth bombers streaked out of the sky and annihilated

Weapons of the War—Cruise Missiles

The Tomahawk cruise missile is one of the most accurate and effective weapons in the high-tech arsenal of the United States. The twenty-foot-long missile has a range of up to fifteen hundred miles. It carries a one-thousand-pound warhead, enough explosives to destroy a factory, bridge, or nearly any military target. Some cruise missiles carry nuclear warheads, but these were not shipped to the Persian Gulf.

The Tomahawk missile is launched from a ship or submarine by a booster rocket. After twelve seconds, a rocket engine on board the missile ignites and powers the weapon. As the missile nears the shore, it "noses down," or flies near ground level, in order to escape enemy radar detection. This takes advantage of the fact that radar beams travel in a straight line, while the surface of the earth is curved. The farther the beams travel from a radar station, the more the ground curves away from them. Thus, a shallow zone is created between beams and ground in which planes can fly undetected.

After the cruise missile reaches the land, a computer guidance system called TERCOM activates. The computer has been programmed with maps and satellite photos of both the terrain below and the target itself. An onboard camera scans the ground and compares what it sees with the images stored in the programmed memory. If the two images do not match, the computer calculates course adjustments and orders the engine to compensate accordingly. This keeps the missile on course. As the weapon approaches the target, the computer recognizes the target and orders the missile to home in on it. The Tomahawk's great speed of 550 miles per hour and its ability to evade enemy radar make it nearly impossible to shoot down or defend against.

(left) A Tomahawk cruise missile is launched from the USS Wisconsin *in the Persian Gulf as Operation Desert Storm commences. (above) This diagram shows the changing trajectory of a cruise missile's flight path.*

Baghdad's night sky is illuminated by exploding bombs from attacking American warplanes during the first wave of Desert Storm.

Iraqi communications facilities, chemical plants, and nuclear research labs. British Tornado jets swooped low over Iraqi airfields, destroying hangars and cratering runways to make them useless. American warships in the Persian Gulf launched more than one hundred Tomahawk cruise missiles equipped with special computerized cameras. These devices were preprogrammed with detailed maps of Iraqi territory. With deadly accuracy, the missiles found and destroyed Iraqi missile sites, oil refineries, and power stations.

In the first few hours, dozens of Allied warplanes converged on Baghdad, striking the defense ministry, the center for Iraqi war efforts, as well as the presidential palace and the airport. Hundreds of Iraqi anti-aircraft guns, many located atop office buildings, opened fire on the attackers. But these guns were almost completely useless against the Allied planes, which flew too high and too fast. The glittering trails of the Iraqi bullets danced in the night sky like a gigantic fireworks display. At the same time, the light from exploding bombs and spreading ground fires illuminated the streets of the Iraqi capital in an eerie glow. Describing the incredible scene from a Baghdad hotel room, CNN reporter Bernard Shaw exclaimed: "Clearly I've never been there, but it feels like we are in the center of hell!" Terrified Iraqi citizens scrambled into air raid shelters or tried to flee the city.

While Allied planes bombed Baghdad, U.S. Apache helicopters prowled the deserts of Kuwait. In the darkness, the helicopters used advanced lasers to locate Iraqi troops, bunkers, and tanks.

Locking onto their targets, the Apaches blasted away with powerful rockets. Farther north, huge American B-52 bombers rained tons of explosives on underground bunkers of Saddam's elite Republican Guards.

During the first day of Desert Storm, the massive Allied air attack took a devastating toll on Iraqi industrial and military facilities. In the first fourteen hours of combat, Allied forces flew more than one thousand sorties, or missions, against Iraqi targets. Hundreds of buildings and dozens of tanks and other vehicles were destroyed. According to U.S. military sources, the Allies pounded Iraq with more than twenty-two hundred tons of explosives in the first twenty-four hours of the air assault. At the end of that first day, with the exception of some ineffective anti-aircraft fire, the Iraqi military still had not managed to mount a counterattack.

Saddam Strikes Back

In a radio broadcast on January 17, one day after the Allied offensive began, Saddam Hussein responded to the Allied attack. But it was not a military response. The Iraqi army continued to offer little or no resistance to the Allied air assault. Instead, Saddam waged a war of words and threats. He called upon all Iraqis to fight back against the "invaders." He announced that the "mother of all battles had begun" and angrily branded President Bush "the Satan of the White House." Saddam also called upon all Arabs to rise up against Iraq's enemies. Attempting to incite international terrorism, he pleaded, "Let the aggressors' interests be set on fire, and let them be hunted down wherever they may be in every corner of the world!" Saddam demanded that Arabs attack the "facilities, symbols and figures" of the United States and its allies. "The time has come," he said, "to crush the enemy and erase the disgrace." But these pleas and demands apparently went unheeded. In the days that followed, no Arab terrorist attacks were reported in the Middle East or elsewhere in the world.

It was on January 18, 1991, that Saddam finally launched a military offensive. His dramatic counterattack shocked people around the world. Following through on his threat to strike out at Israel, he ordered a missile attack against the Israelis at about 2:00 A.M. Detecting the incoming "Scud" missiles, Israeli defense systems sounded warning sirens. Saddam had warned months before that he would "burn half" of Israel with chemical weapons, and the Israelis were prepared for a poison gas attack. Israeli citizens immediately donned gas masks, which the government had distributed in the weeks leading up to the U.N. deadline.

People in the United States and other countries tensely watched live broadcasts of the Israelis waiting for the missiles to

Gen. Norman Schwarzkopf

Norman Schwarzkopf, commander of the coalition forces of operations Desert Shield and Desert Storm, attended West Point Military Academy in the 1950s. He later served two tours of duty as a junior officer in the Vietnam War. It was there that he risked his life crossing a mine field to rescue a GI whose leg had been blown off by a mine. It was also in Vietnam that Schwarzkopf picked up the nickname "Stormin' Norman," which he claims to hate. He prefers what most of his staff members call him—"the bear."

Schwarzkopf's military colleagues say he is a good soldier who knows how to weigh a situation and get a job done. They credit him with putting together the right blend of armor, artillery, and air power in the Gulf War operations. Military experts say he did an excellent job of coordinating the armed forces of the many countries in the Allied coalition. Former marine Commandant P. X. Kelley called Schwarzkopf "a superb strategist, a brilliant tactician [goal achiever], tough as nails and a real troop handler."

Schwarzkopf is known for his bluntness. In the weeks leading up to the Gulf War, he referred to the Iraqi generals as "a bunch of thugs" and promised to "kick [Saddam's] butt." Balancing this image of the hardened soldier, say Schwarzkopf's friends, "the bear" is unusually cultured and well rounded. He speaks fluent French and German and enjoys ballet and opera. He is also a devoted family man who performed magic shows at his children's birthday parties.

Allied commander Gen. H. Norman Schwarzkopf jokes with troops as they await the order to go into action.

fall. Suddenly, about twenty minutes after the missile alert had begun, eight Scuds roared out of the early morning darkness. Two smashed into Israel's capital, Tel Aviv, while three struck the port city of Haifa. The other three Iraqi missiles landed in open fields. Ambulances, fire fighters, and military personnel that rushed to the impact sites found a great deal of property damage but few casualties. The highly inaccurate Scuds had struck randomly, causing no fatalities and only fifteen injuries.

(left) Israeli kindergartners don gas masks to practice for the eventuality of an Iraqi chemical weapons attack. (above) An Israeli soldier uses a specially trained dog to search for buried victims after an Iraqi Scud missile attack on Tel Aviv.

The attack on Israel brought cries of outrage from people around the world. Israel, which was not a member of the Allied coalition, had not provoked the assault. And the Iraqis were hitting civilian rather than military targets, a clear violation of international law. Israelis interviewed on camera called Saddam a barbarian and a madman. Many people all over the world agreed.

Because Israel is known for its swift counterattacks, people around the world were surprised and relieved when Israel did not immediately retaliate against the Iraqis. The Israelis held back at the request of President Bush. Even as the Scuds were falling on Israel, Bush pleaded with Israeli leaders not to retaliate. He feared that an Israeli attack on Iraq would enrage all Arabs and that the Saudis and Egyptians might then abandon the Allied operation. Bush offered to retaliate for the Israelis by hunting down the Scud launchers in western Iraq.

The Israelis were reluctant to stand by and do nothing while their country was attacked. But they decided to refrain from retaliating, partly in response to pleas from the United States and other Western allies to do so. The Israelis also hoped that their restraint would send a signal to all Arabs that Israel wanted peace. This might lead to better Arab-Israeli relations in the future.

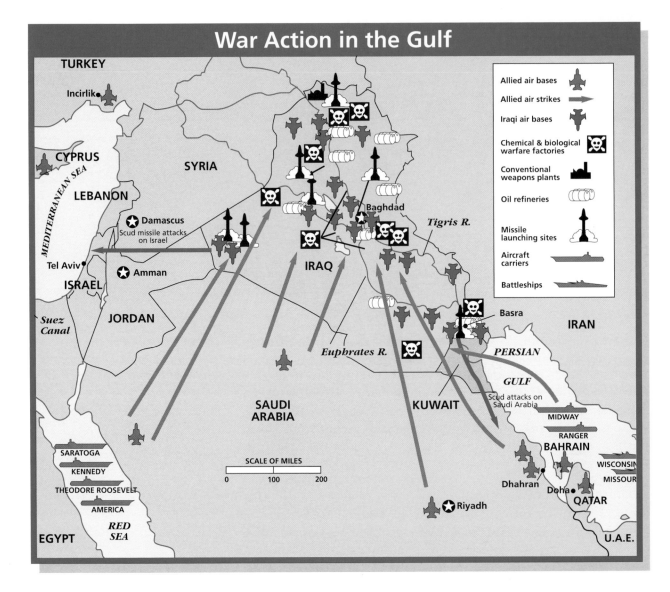

War Action in the Gulf

Legend:
- Allied air bases
- Allied air strikes
- Iraqi air bases
- Chemical & biological warfare factories
- Conventional weapons plants
- Oil refineries
- Missile launching sites
- Aircraft carriers
- Battleships

Map labels: TURKEY, Incirlik, CYPRUS, MEDITERRANEAN SEA, SYRIA, LEBANON, Damascus, Scud missile attacks on Israel, Tel Aviv, ISRAEL, Amman, JORDAN, Suez Canal, Baghdad, Tigris R., IRAQ, Euphrates R., SAUDI ARABIA, SARATOGA, KENNEDY, THEODORE ROOSEVELT, AMERICA, EGYPT, RED SEA, SCALE OF MILES 0 100 200, Riyadh, KUWAIT, Scud attacks on Saudi Arabia, Basra, IRAN, PERSIAN GULF, MIDWAY, RANGER, BAHRAIN, WISCONSIN, MISSOURI, Dhahran, Doha, QATAR, U.A.E.

Desperate and Irrational Acts

While launching missiles against Israel, the Iraqis also attacked Saudi Arabia. But their efforts were random, uncoordinated, and largely ineffective. Allied military commanders expressed the view that Saddam was desperately trying to show the world that he could fight back. But he had no overall plan. Also, his air force had already been eliminated from the war, and most of his tanks were hidden in desert bunkers to avoid Allied bombers. Saddam's only available major offensive weapons were a few Scud missiles and some large artillery guns scattered across southern Iraq and Kuwait.

First, the Iraqis fired some of their artillery, but most of the shells fell harmlessly into the Saudi desert. Their only direct hit was on the Saudi oil facility at Kafji on the gulf coast. Sections of

Weapons of the War—Patriots Versus Scuds

All through the air war in the Persian Gulf, the world's attention was riveted on a dramatic duel in the skies above the Middle East. This battle was not fought between airplanes, but between deadly missiles.

Early in the conflict, Saddam Hussein began firing his Soviet-made SS-1 missiles, nicknamed "Scuds," into Saudi Arabia and Israel. Originally, the Scuds, which carry a two-thousand-pound warhead, had a range, or traveling distance, of only 186 miles. The Iraqis managed to make improvements, which extended that range to almost 500 miles. This made the missiles a threat to much of the Middle East, including Israel.

However, the Scuds are very inaccurate and often miss their intended targets by as much as several miles. According to military experts, this makes the Scuds an insignificant military threat. The missiles are primarily terror weapons. They create an atmosphere of tension and fear because no one can be sure where they might fall. The Allies could not eliminate the Scud menace simply by bombing the missiles' launch pads. Many of the Scud launchers were mobile, carried from place to place on the backs of large trucks. The Iraqis were able to hide these launchers from Allied planes and continue firing missiles.

The United States countered the Scud attacks with its sophisticated Patriot air defense system. A Patriot missile station consists of a launcher equipped with four missiles and a mobile, or easily movable, radar trailer. After an enemy Scud missile is launched, the Patriot system's radar tracks the flight of the Scud. A Patriot antimissile missile is then fired. An advanced guidance system in the missile exchanges information with the computers in the radar trailer, allowing the Patriot to home in on the incoming Scud. As the two weapons near each other, the Patriot explodes into a shower of lethal metal fragments that destroy the Scud.

(left) A Patriot antimissile follows a computer-assisted course to intercept an incoming missile. (below) A diagram shows how a Patriot missile, released from a launcher, intercepts an incoming Scud.

The laserlike trail of a Patriot missile splits the sky over Tel Aviv on its way to intercept and destroy an incoming Scud missile.

A Saudi Arabian government officer examines an oil-slicked seabird. Hundreds of birds were killed after Iraqi forces in Kuwait deliberately spilled oil into the Persian Gulf.

the facility exploded and caught fire, sending an ominous plume of black smoke skyward. But the plant was not destroyed, and the attack had no effect on the Allied offensive. A few hours later, an Iraqi Scud missile homed in on the Allied air base at Dhahran. Moments before impact, U.S. forces fired a radar-guided Patriot antimissile missile, destroying the Scud in midair. As the explosion lit up the night sky, Allied troops cheered and applauded.

This was the first time that the Patriots had been used in war, and they had proven to be highly effective against incoming missiles. After this initial success, U.S. commanders decided to ship several Patriot units to Israel to help defend against further Scud attacks on that country. Israeli officials welcomed the missiles since more Iraqi Scuds fell on Israel on January 19 while the Patriots were being set up. Once again, there was extensive property damage but few casualties. During the next several days, while the Israelis trained to use the Patriots, American technicians operated the missiles.

Saddam continued with his largely ineffective Scud attacks out of necessity. Without his air force, and faced with Allied planes firing relentlessly at military targets, he was unable to mount a standard counterattack using planes and tanks. For this reason, Saddam followed up the Scud attacks with other desperate and unconventional tactics. For example, on January 23, the Iraqis began releasing oil from their storage tanks directly into the gulf. At the rate of more than four million gallons a day, the black tide expanded southward, killing thousands of birds and other animals. U.S. officials called the deliberate oil spill "sick," "irrational," and an act of "environmental terrorism." They theorized that Saddam released the oil in order to clog up and close down a Saudi desalination plant that converts sea water into fresh water. Saudi and American engineers quickly erected barriers around the facility, and the oil failed to damage the plant's machines.

Assault on Kafji

On January 29, 1991, Iraqi forces sped over the border into Saudi Arabia, crossed six miles of desert, and seized control of the small town of Kafji. The town, built along a Persian Gulf beach, had been abandoned since the August 2 Iraqi invasion of Kuwait. U.S. military experts guessed that Saddam was trying to impress Middle Eastern Arabs by launching a ground attack, however small, on Saudi Arabia. But the Allies were surprised and perplexed that the Iraqis entered enemy territory without the protection of fighter planes. Such protection is standard procedure in modern offensive warfare. Remarked former U.S. Army colonel David H. Hackworth, "For Iraq to send in armor without air cover—and in this war they'll never have air cover—was suicidal....It was an operation doomed from the start." Thus, it appeared that Saddam was willing to send his men to almost certain death in an attempt to bolster his own image.

After the Iraqis entered the town, Allied forces quickly surrounded Kafji, and opened fire on the Iraqis. At the same time, gunboats in the gulf and attack jets overhead unleashed a barrage of explosives on Iraqi positions. After several hours, the big guns ceased firing, and Saudi troops moved into the town. The sounds of automatic weapons and grenade explosions echoed during the furious house-to-house fighting that followed. The Saudis, defending their homeland, pressed forward relentlessly, forcing the Iraqis to give up street after street.

Finally, after holding the town for just thirty-six hours, most of the Iraqi tanks and men turned and fled north toward the border. They left behind thirty dead and another 429 of their comrades stranded in the town. These stragglers, exhausted and frightened, wasted no time in surrendering to the Saudis. Eighteen Saudi soldiers died in the battle. Said Colonel Hackworth, "Saddam Hussein says 'the mother of all battles' awaits the Allies, and will turn defeat into victory....If this was the mother of battles or even one of its offspring, then it died at birth."

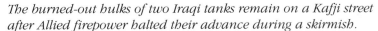

The burned-out hulks of two Iraqi tanks remain on a Kafji street after Allied firepower halted their advance during a skirmish.

Another ineffective and seemingly irrational Iraqi maneuver occurred a few days later. On January 29, several thousand Iraqi troops suddenly crossed the border into Saudi Arabia and occupied the abandoned town of Kafji on the gulf shore. This move made no sense from a military standpoint because the town had no strategic significance. U.S. military experts suggested that Saddam was desperately trying to show his Arab supporters that his army could go on the offensive. But the offensive was short-lived, for Allied forces instantly surrounded and shelled the Iraqis in Kafji. Saudi soldiers then moved into the town, inflicting heavy casualties and taking nearly five hundred Iraqi prisoners. Allied military commanders called the Iraqi attack "suicidal" and a "humiliating defeat."

Countdown to the Ground Attack

U.S. Air Force medical personnel cheer on a fighter pilot taking off for a bombing run over Iraq.

Meanwhile, Allied bombing missions against Iraq continued at the rate of thousands per day. Allied warplanes destroyed

bridges, airfields, and military centers. Iraq's two operating nuclear power plants were leveled. By early February 1991, the 4.5 million people of Baghdad had almost no electricity or running water. Hundreds of Iraqi tanks and trucks had become charred, twisted hulks littering the desert. Most of Iraq's military and industrial facilities were in ruins. Tens of thousands of Iraqi military personnel were dead, while Allied fatalities still numbered less than one hundred.

Despite the widespread destruction and misery the air war had brought to his country, Saddam stubbornly refused to order his forces out of Kuwait. On February 22, President Bush delivered a dramatic public warning to the Iraqi dictator. Saddam had to begin withdrawing from Kuwait by noon on February 23 or face a devastating ground assault by Allied forces. Once more, people around the world held their breaths. Some remembered the tough, ominous words of top-ranking U.S. general Colin Powell. In January, he had told reporters how the Allies would defeat the Iraqi army in Kuwait. "First," said Powell, "we're going to cut it off [from its supply lines], then we're going to kill it." After weeks of bombing, the Iraqis in Kuwait were, as Powell predicted, cut off and isolated. Now, apparently, it was time for the Allies to move in for the kill.

CHAPTER SIX

One Hundred Hours— The Allied Ground Offensive

An American infantryman practices trench warfare—desert-style—in preparation for an Allied ground assault on Iraqi forces in Kuwait.

The ground attack by Allied troops began at 8:00 P.M. on February 23, 1991. President Bush announced the beginning of this attack two hours later, saying that Iraq had not met the Allied demand to leave Kuwait. Bush explained that he had ordered General Schwarzkopf "to use all forces available, including ground forces, to eject the Iraqi army from Kuwait."

Allied Forces Sweep into Iraq

The overall plan of the Allied attack was to move troops northward into southeastern Iraq and cut off Kuwait from the rest of Iraq. Then the Allies would concentrate on defeating Iraqi forces in Kuwait. The assault relied partly on deception. For weeks preceding the attack, the Allied commanders had kept most of their forces massed in the Saudi desert south of Kuwait. This led the Iraqis to believe that the main thrust of an Allied attack would push northward into Kuwait. But at the last minute, the Allies shifted most of their troops and tanks toward the west, south of Iraq. The Iraqis were not aware of these changes. They did not have spotter airplanes to keep them informed of enemy troop movements. General Schwarzkopf also stationed eighteen thousand U.S. Marines in plain sight in the Persian Gulf near the Kuwaiti coast. Thinking that there would be an amphibious assault, or attack over water, the Iraqis pulled thousands of troops out of the desert and placed them near the coast.

Thus, the Iraqis were taken completely by surprise when the bulk of the Allied forces swept northward into Iraq. It was in southeastern Iraq near the Kuwaiti border that the Republican Guards had constructed hundreds of underground concrete bunkers. Saddam Hussein had been holding these, his best troops, in reserve. If an Allied ground offensive swept northward through Kuwait, he reasoned, the Republican Guards would keep the enemy from entering Iraq. Now, unbeknownst to the guards, thousands of American tanks and armored vehicles, accompanied by tens of thousands of American and British troops, sped through the desert. Within a few hours, they penetrated deeply into Iraq and moved toward the rear of the heavily armored guard positions.

At the same time, farther west, hundreds of American helicopters and French troops streaked across southern and central Iraq. They quickly established well-guarded supply bases in the desert, then hurried north to the Euphrates River. There, they stood ready to stop a possible Iraqi retreat along the river. These moves completely cut off Kuwait and southeastern Iraq from the rest of Iraq. Saddam's armies in and near Kuwait were trapped.

The Assault on Kuwait

While Allied troops swept into Iraq, a combined force of Americans, Saudis, Egyptians, and Syrians launched a lightning assault into southern Kuwait. Hundreds of tanks rolled across the border and opened fire on Iraqi desert positions. More than fifty thousand Allied soldiers followed the tanks. They were tense, ready to throw on their gas masks and chemical protection gear at a moment's notice. But the Iraqi chemical attack many had feared did not come. In fact, to the surprise of Allied soldiers, there was little resistance of any kind from Iraqi troops in southern Kuwait.

U.S. Marines train for a possible ground war during Operation Desert Shield.

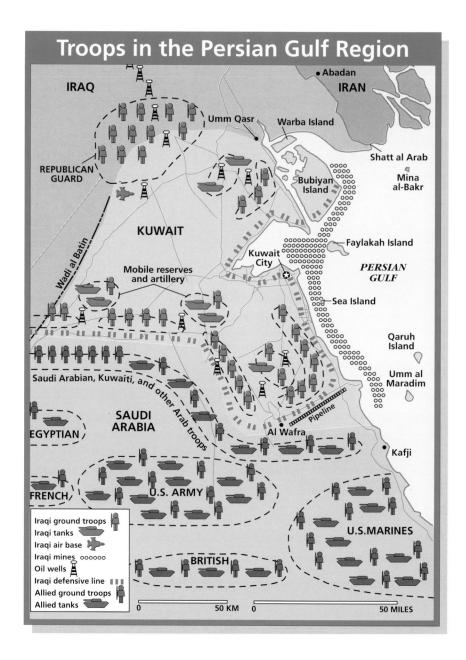

Troops in the Persian Gulf Region

IRAQ

IRAN

Abadan

Umm Qasr

Warba Island

Shatt al Arab

REPUBLICAN GUARD

Bubiyan Island

Mina al-Bakr

KUWAIT

Faylakah Island

Kuwait City

PERSIAN GULF

Wadi al Batin

Mobile reserves and artillery

Sea Island

Qaruh Island

Umm al Maradim

Saudi Arabian, Kuwaiti, and other Arab troops

Pipeline

EGYPTIAN

SAUDI ARABIA

Al Wafra

Kafji

FRENCH

U.S. ARMY

U.S. MARINES

BRITISH

Iraqi ground troops
Iraqi tanks
Iraqi air base
Iraqi mines oooooo
Oil wells
Iraqi defensive line
Allied ground troops
Allied tanks

0   50 KM   0   50 MILES

Most of the Iraqis in the desert along the Kuwaiti-Saudi border had already been battered into submission by weeks of Allied bombing raids. Hour after hour, day after day, the massive air assaults had pounded the Iraqi positions. Waves of huge U.S. B-52 bombers glided low and released their deadly cargoes of explosives on the Iraqi bunkers and trenches. Tanks, trucks, and other objects above ground were reduced to charred masses of twisted metal.

For the Iraqi soldiers crowded inside the dark, dusty underground bunkers, it was like a nightmare that would never end. With each new explosion, the ground heaved to and fro, covering

Weapons of the War—American High-Tech Ground Weapons

The primary U.S. ground weapon of the Gulf War was the M-1A1 Abrams tank. Called by some military experts "the high-tech tank of all time," the fifty-five-ton M-1A1 fires a special nonnuclear shell called a uranium bolt. The shell can travel up to two miles and penetrate the armor of conventional enemy tanks. By contrast, the shells from most foreign-made tanks cannot penetrate the M-1A1's armor. Each M-1A1, costing $4.4 million to build in 1990, is equipped with an array of advanced devices designed to protect the crew from nuclear, chemical, and biological attacks. For instance, once the entry hatch is closed, the inside of the tank is sealed with special materials that keep even germs from penetrating. These seals will not corrode or break down when exposed to harmful chemicals. In addition, the vehicle carries food, medical equipment, and other life-support systems designed to keep the crew alive inside for several days. The tank is also outfitted with special infrared scopes that allow it to maneuver at night.

Another high-tech U.S. ground weapon is the Copperhead, a laser-guided antitank device. The Copperhead's laser systems provide near-pinpoint accuracy for its powerful shells, which cost fifty thousand dollars each. Also in the U.S. arsenal: the Quick Fix helicopter, designed to jam and confuse enemy radio communications, and the Mobile Subscriber Equipment, or MSE, a giant computerized communications system that links more than ten thousand U.S. battle radios at one time.

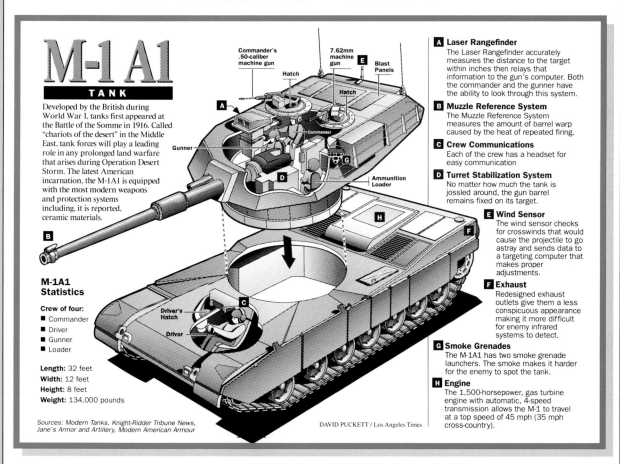

M-1A1 TANK

Developed by the British during World War I, tanks first appeared at the Battle of the Somme in 1916. Called "chariots of the desert" in the Middle East, tank forces will play a leading role in any prolonged land warfare that arises during Operation Desert Storm. The latest American incarnation, the M-1A1 is equipped with the most modern weapons and protection systems including, it is reported, ceramic materials.

M-1A1 Statistics

Crew of four:
- Commander
- Driver
- Gunner
- Loader

Length: 32 feet
Width: 12 feet
Height: 8 feet
Weight: 134,000 pounds

Sources: Modern Tanks, Knight-Ridder Tribune News, Jane's Armor and Artillery, Modern American Armour

DAVID PUCKETT / Los Angeles Times

Commander's .50-caliber machine gun
Hatch
7.62mm machine gun
Blast Panels
Hatch
Commander
Gunner
Ammunition Loader
Driver's Hatch
Driver

A Laser Rangefinder
The Laser Rangefinder accurately measures the distance to the target within inches then relays that information to the gun's computer. Both the commander and the gunner have the ability to look through this system.

B Muzzle Reference System
The Muzzle Reference System measures the amount of barrel warp caused by the heat of repeated firing.

C Crew Communications
Each of the crew has a headset for easy communication

D Turret Stabilization System
No matter how much the tank is jossled around, the gun barrel remains fixed on its target.

E Wind Sensor
The wind sensor checks for crosswinds that would cause the projectile to go astray and sends data to a targeting computer that makes proper adjustments.

F Exhaust
Redesigned exhaust outlets give them a less conspicuous appearance making it more difficult for enemy infrared systems to detect.

G Smoke Grenades
The M-1A1 has two smoke grenade launchers. The smoke makes it harder for the enemy to spot the tank.

H Engine
The 1,500-horsepower, gas turbine engine with automatic, 4-speed transmission allows the M-1 to travel at a top speed of 45 mph (35 mph cross-country).

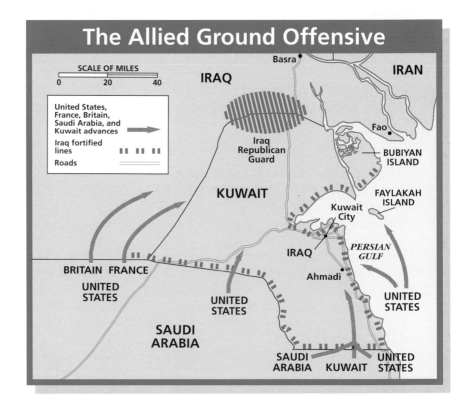

The Allied Ground Offensive

everything with showers of sand and debris. The deafening blasts made it nearly impossible to sleep or even to think clearly. Each time a bunker received a direct hit, dozens of soldiers died instantly, their bodies torn to shreds by the force of the impact. And every hour or so, the bombing would cause a cavern or bunker to collapse, burying its occupants alive. There was little food or water, for the Allied bombing campaign had cut off most supply lines. There was also little news from the outside world. Most of the Iraqi troops caught in the relentless rain of explosives received no reports about the events of the war. And after weeks of what seemed like a living hell, many no longer cared. All that many wanted to do was get out of these holes of death and go home.

Most of these weary, frightened, and starving Iraqis chose surrender rather than certain death. As the Allies approached, white flags popped up from bunkers and trenches all along the Iraqi defensive lines. More than five thousand Iraqi soldiers surrendered in the first twenty hours of the ground war. Thousands more gave up in each succeeding hour. Iraqi officers had told them that the Americans were barbarians who would torture and then shoot them. So, many Iraqis crawled on their knees toward American soldiers, crying openly and begging for their lives. They grabbed and kissed the hands of astonished American GIs, who could only look with pity upon their defeated and bedraggled enemies.

Anxious to Surrender

Starving and exhausted after weeks of Allied bombing raids, tens of thousands of Iraqi soldiers in southern Kuwait surrendered during the one-hundred-hour ground war. Many Iraqis were so anxious to surrender that they gave themselves up to any foreigners they encountered. On February 28, 1991, about a dozen Iraqi soldiers approached an Italian news crew covering the war in the desert. The Iraqis waved white flags and held their hands in the air. When it became clear that the Italians would not shoot them, the smiling Iraqis chanted such phrases as "We salute Italy!" and "God smile on Italy!" in broken Italian. The journalists then gave their prisoners crackers and water, the first meal many of the Iraqis had enjoyed in days. Repeatedly cursing Saddam Hussein, the prisoners explained how they had fled their trenches and walked eighteen miles in order to surrender. About an hour later, fourteen more Iraqis surrendered to the same Italian crew. Later that day, the journalists wished their prisoners good luck as they handed them over to members of the Red Cross. In all, more than a hundred Iraqis gave themselves up to news crews from various nations.

(above) Iraqi prisoners of war march through the Kuwaiti desert after being captured by Allied forces. (right) Many Iraqi soldiers surrendered before engaging Allied troops.

Captured Iraqi soldiers await transport out of Kuwait as an Allied tank crew stands guard.

With so little Iraqi resistance in southern Kuwait, the way was clear for an Allied push toward Kuwait's capital. Tens of thousands of Allied troops, spearheaded by American, Saudi, and Kuwaiti forces, moved northward. Tanks of the American Tiger Brigade raced to the west of the city to cut off any Iraqis trying to escape.

Rampage and Massacre

Aware that the Allies were approaching, frightened Iraqi troops in Kuwait City went on a rampage. For reasons unknown, they burned many houses and businesses, raped Kuwaiti women, and looted homes and stores. "They took everything," a Kuwaiti woman later recalled: "televisions, radios, food, even dog food." Thinking that the Allies would take at least a day or two to reach the city, the Iraqis continued their looting and destruction for many hours. They then loaded their booty into cars, trucks, school buses, and any other vehicles they could find. Their plan was to escape along Kuwait's northern highway, which led from Kuwait City to the southern Iraqi city of Basra. But they had waited too long. A long line of Tiger Brigade tanks approached the city, destroying any moving vehicles in their path.

In a wild panic, the Iraqis dashed for the highway, but so many thousands tried to escape at once, a massive traffic jam formed. In the early morning hours of February 26, the U.S. tanks came within range of the miles-long Iraqi convoy. Allied pilots also spotted the escaping vehicles and moved in for the kill. Journalist Tony Clifton, aboard one of the tanks, described the attack as a massacre, looking like "something out of a medieval artist's vision of hell." As the tanks and planes blasted away, said Clifton, the highway became "a great backdrop of leaping flames against which we could see the tiny figures of men frantically trying to escape the fire."

Hours later, the highway was a graveyard of corpses and burned vehicles. Said Clifton,

> As we drove slowly through the wreckage...[we] splashed through great pools of bloody water. We passed dead soldiers lying as if resting, without a mark on them. We found others cut up so badly, a pair of legs in its trousers would be 50 yards from the top half of the body.... Most grotesque of all was the charred corpse of an Iraqi tank crewman, his blackened arms stretched upward in a sort of supplication [prayer].

Kuwait City Liberated

At nearby Kuwait City airport, Iraqi soldiers attempted to repulse the invading Allies. U.S. Marines poured into the airport, quickly encircled the Iraqis, then closed in as if tightening a noose. Many Iraqis died as they ran from one building to another seeking cover. Eventually, seeing that their situation was hopeless, the surviving Iraqi defenders gave up. In the next few hours, other Iraqis tried to escape through the desert, but Allied forces killed or captured them. Thousands of Iraqis died in the vicinity of Kuwait City, and many thousands more were wounded or captured. In the three days of fighting to retake the capital and airport, the Americans counted only five dead and forty-eight injured. Other Allied casualties were also light.

On February 27, less than four days after the ground offensive began, Allied forces moved into Kuwait City, now largely

A U.S. Special Forces trooper searches a section of Kuwait City house by house looking for remaining Iraqi soldiers.

A motorist in Dubai, United Arab Emirates, holds up headlines that announce the liberation of Kuwait.

free of Iraqi troops. The Americans waited on the outskirts of the city, allowing the Kuwaiti and other Arab forces to go in first and officially reclaim the capital. When the Americans entered a few hours later, thousands of jubilant Kuwaitis greeted them. Kuwaiti citizens leaped up onto tanks and trucks and kissed the American soldiers. The Kuwaitis shouted their thanks to President Bush and the other Allied leaders. Then they screamed, "Down with Saddam!" and burned paintings of the dictator that the Iraqis had erected in city squares. People everywhere fired rifles into the air to celebrate the freeing of the city.

Iraq's Army Is Crushed

Although Kuwait City had been liberated, the war was not over yet. The large force of Republican Guards in southeastern Iraq was still intact. The Allies had to eliminate this threat before Kuwait would be safe from Iraqi attack.

On February 27, 1991, while American and Arab forces were liberating Kuwait, the largest tank battle since World War II was about to begin in southern Iraq. The massive U.S. Army Seventh Corps closed in on the Republican Guards. The Seventh's more than one thousand tanks and armored carriers and tens of thousands of men had traveled nearly two hundred miles in less than three days. This operation was made possible by an enormous, perfectly coordinated supply effort involving thousands of U.S. helicopters and trucks. Each day, they ferried five thousand tons of ammunition, 555,000 gallons of fuel, 300,000 gallons of water, and eighty thousand meals into the battle zone.

After Kuwait's liberation, jubilant Kuwaitis take their country's flag from a captured Iraqi tank.

Unlike their countrymen in southern Kuwait, most of the Republican Guards were ready to put up a stiff fight. The guard forces consisted of more than three hundred tanks and nearly sixty thousand men, most battle hardened in the Iraq-Iran war. But, like other Iraqi forces, the guards were surprised when the Americans swung around through southern Iraq and approached Iraqi positions from behind.

In the desert fifteen miles west of Basra, Iraq's second largest city, the two armies clashed. The American tanks drew up in a miles-long curved line around the guard positions and opened fire. The Iraqis returned fire as best they could. But they were not as well trained in maneuvering large groups of tanks as were the Allies. Also, the Iraqis' aging, Soviet-made T-55 tanks were no match for the more than eight hundred U.S. M-1A1 high-tech tanks that began to close in on them. With deadly precision, advanced laser systems on the M-1A1s guided shells to direct hits on Iraqi tanks, trucks, and artillery.

At the same time, U.S. Apache helicopters and A-10 attack planes pounded the Iraqis from the air. The Iraqi tanks exploded into huge fireballs, sending metal fragments, some weighing tons, flying in every direction. Most of the Republican Guards inside the tanks were instantly burned to death. The few who survived these hits, their clothes and hair aflame, ran screaming across the sands and into hails of U.S. rockets and machine gun bullets. More guards poured from the bunkers and fired their machine guns at the Allies. But their efforts had little effect on the massive and well-coordinated array of tanks and aircraft that bore down on them.

Women Soldiers in the Gulf

Mom, if you die over there, I'm coming to rescue you," said Lt. Col. Carolyn Roaf's daughter as they said good-bye. Roaf was on her way with thousands of other American women soldiers to serve in the Persian Gulf. Women have taken part in all U.S. wars. But, as journalist Melinda Beck reports, never "on such a large scale or in such a wide variety of jobs."

Of the two million people serving in the U.S. armed forces in 1990, 11 percent were women. Women make up 7 percent of U.S. sailors and army gun crews, 10 percent of secret intelligence gatherers, as well as 35 percent of administrators.

And nearly 10 percent of the military's officers are women. In Saudi Arabia, women pilots flew helicopters carrying troops and supplies, and women mechanics maintained tanks and trucks. Women also served as ship navigators, communications experts, and paratroopers, or parachute jumpers.

According to U.S. law, women still cannot take part in actual combat, but commanders no longer remove them from dangerous areas when fighting begins. "Just because you're not in a combat unit," said a former Defense Department official, "doesn't mean you won't be in combat. When they [the Iraqis] start lobbing Scuds with chemical weapons, they'll be aiming at everybody." The dangers faced by women serving in Operation Desert Storm became clear in early February 1991. U.S. patrols found an abandoned American truck near the Saudi-Kuwaiti border. Two GIs were missing, one of them twenty-year-old Melissa Rathbun-Nealy from Newaygo, Michigan. She was later released along with other American POWs.

Women soldiers insist that they should receive no special treatment because they are women. They say that they are doing their jobs just like the men and are willing to take the same risks. But many Americans still hold onto traditional ideas about protecting women. Explained *Newsweek*'s Tom Morganthau, "The question is how the public will react to seeing women held captive—and possibly tortured—by the enemy. For women in the military, attaining equality may carry a terrible price."

A woman marine arrives at a Saudi Arabian air base during Operation Desert Shield. Thousands of other servicewomen took part in the Persian Gulf War.

By the morning of February 28, after more than ten hours of bloody combat, the surviving guards surrendered. Thousands of Iraqis lay dead amid the smashed remains of more than two hundred of their tanks. Fewer than twenty Americans died, and no U.S. tanks were destroyed in the battle. As U.S. troops rounded up the Iraqi prisoners, President Bush announced on television, "Kuwait is liberated. Iraq's army is defeated. Our military objectives are met. America and the world drew a line in the sand. We declared that the aggression against Kuwait would not stand, and tonight America and the world have kept their word."

(left) Smoke billows from a power plant destroyed by Iraqi forces in Kuwait City. (above) Despite seeing her hometown in ruins, a Kuwait City resident cheerfully flashes a smile and the victory sign.

Kuwait Devastated

In just one hundred hours, the Allied ground offensive had cut off Kuwait from Iraq, freed the Kuwaiti people, and crushed the Iraqi army. During the forty-three-day war, the Iraqis counted an estimated 50,000 dead, another 50,000 or more wounded, and more than 125,000 captured. By comparison, the combined Allied forces suffered only 177 killed, 597 wounded, and fewer than 60 taken prisoner.

At a briefing held for reporters in Saudi Arabia, General Schwarzkopf gave much of the credit for the overwhelming Allied victory to the soldiers who fought in the desert. Calling them "heroes" and their performances "brilliant," he said that "we ought to be very, very proud of them." The Allied commander blamed the quick collapse of Iraq's forces on poor leadership, specifically singling out Saddam. "As far as Saddam Hussein being a great military strategist," said Schwarzkopf, "he is neither a strategist, nor is he schooled in the operational arts, nor is he a tactician, nor is he a general, nor is he a soldier. Other than that," Schwarzkopf added with a grin, "he is a great military man, I want you to know that."

Though the Allied victory was total, it was partly overshadowed by the devastation the Iraqi occupiers had wrought on Kuwait and its people. Apparently out of sheer hatred and cruelty, the Iraqis killed thousands of Kuwaitis and tortured many more. During the months of Iraqi occupation, Kuwait's four major medical centers accumulated the corpses of dozens of Kuwaitis who had been mutilated by Iraqi soldiers. There were many bodies with ax wounds, ears cut off, eyes gouged out, intestines inflated with air, and skulls sawed in half. The Iraqis beat thousands of innocent people, raped hundreds of Kuwaiti women, looted stores, burned buildings, and transported truckloads of Kuwaiti property to Iraq. They stole televisions, appliances, printing presses, street lamps, college libraries, and museum artifacts. They destroyed hotels and government buildings, including the Kuwaiti parliament. They also trashed the emir's palace, smearing the floors with human excrement.

The Iraqis continued their destruction even after the ground war began. When they knew defeat was imminent, they instituted a "scorched earth" policy, the systematic destruction of the things the enemy would find most valuable. Teams of Iraqi soldiers set ablaze more than 600 of Kuwait's 950 oil wells. Thick columns of smoke and dust blotted out the sun, creating twilight at noon across much of Kuwait. These wells continued to burn out of control and some experts expect them to continue to burn for as long as two years.

Horrified by this wanton destruction, the Allies issued stern demands, which the Iraqis had to accept in order to bring about a permanent cease-fire. President Bush made it plain that the present halt in the Allied bombing of Iraq might be temporary. He warned that the Allies could and would resume the war immediately and with punishing effect if the Iraqis did not agree to Allied terms. First, said Bush, the Iraqis must immediately free all Allied prisoners of war. Allied planes, ships, and ground forces remained on full alert, waiting to see if this initial demand would be met.

"Aggression Is Defeated"— Working for a Middle East Peace

The Allied coalition, led by U.S. forces, had won an impressive victory over the Iraqi army. President Bush, his popularity in the United States still soaring because of his handling of the war, addressed a televised joint session of Congress on March 6. He received a thunderous standing ovation after announcing, "Aggression is defeated...the war is over." The president gave credit for the victory to the soldiers. "This victory belongs to them," he declared—"to the privates and the pilots, to the sergeants and the supply officers...to the finest fighting force this nation has ever known. We went halfway around the world to do what is moral and just and right. And we fought hard and, with others, we won the war [to lift] the yoke of tyranny and aggression from a small country that many Americans had never even heard of.... Thank you guys, thank you very, very much!"

Bush put into words what most Americans felt. The U.S. all-volunteer army of regular and reserve soldiers had proved itself to be a well-coordinated and superior fighting force. When called upon to go to war, these men and women had performed their jobs efficiently, professionally, and courageously. Years after Vietnam, Americans once more had confidence in their military and pride in their country. Said President Bush at a White House meeting, "By God, we've kicked the Vietnam syndrome [loser image] once and for all!" Evidence of the truth of these words came when U.S. troops began returning home from the Persian Gulf. The soldiers received triumphant heroes' welcomes, in contrast to Vietnam veterans who were either criticized or ignored. Excited crowds greeted the Gulf War soldiers as they arrived home on

A returning U.S. Marine is greeted by his wife and baby son at Camp Pendleton, California.

(left) Victorious troops are the guests of honor at a ticker-tape parade in New York City on June 10, 1991. (right) About ten thousand people join in a rally at Georgia Tech's football stadium in Atlanta to show support for U.S. troops in the Persian Gulf. Unlike the Vietnam War, the majority of American people supported the war effort in the Gulf.

planes and ships. There were parades in their honor all over the nation. In addition, President Bush asked that special celebrations be held for the returning heroes on July 4, 1991.

Almost everything in the war had gone in the Allies' favor. In particular, many of the dire predictions voiced by diplomats, military experts, and war critics before the war began never came true. Some had warned that it would be a long war, that Saddam would draw the United States and its allies into another costly and draining Vietnam. But the total Allied victory came in only forty-three days. Others said that Saddam's huge battle-hardened army would inflict heavy casualties on the Allies, weakening the spirit and resolve of the Western countries. But most Iraqi troops, ill equipped and supplied, badly led, and lacking in morale, either surrendered or offered only token resistance.

Other feared events did not happen. Many people were sure that the Iraqis would use chemical weapons, adding a terrifying dimension to the conflict. But Iraqi commanders held back, fearing the Allies would respond in kind. And Saddam's much-feared pan-Arab jihad, a worldwide wave of terrorism, never came to pass. According to U.S. officials, many would-be terrorists concluded that Saddam's was a lost cause or were discouraged by tight security measures around the globe.

In spite of these victories, many people in the United States, including several members of Congress, felt the win was incomplete because the Allies had failed to remove Saddam Hussein from power. This would make it impossible for the Iraqi people to form a new, more democratic government. There seemed little doubt that Saddam would continue to rule his country with an iron hand. But most people in the West were at least confident that the war had weakened Saddam enough to keep him from further threatening the peace of the region. From the Allied point of view, the war's achievements greatly overshadowed its failures.

The Fruits of Victory

The Allies had been so successful that they were in a position to dictate whatever cease-fire terms they wanted to the Iraqis. General Schwarzkopf set the time and place of a meeting between Allied and Iraqi commanders. On March 3, 1991, a bit less than six days after the fighting had ceased, they met at a captured Iraqi airfield in Safwan near the Iraqi-Kuwaiti border. The tent in which the meeting took place was surrounded by more than fifty tanks draped in U.S. and British flags. General Schwarzkopf made an impressive entrance, arriving in a squadron of six Apache attack helicopters. Two Iraqi generals appeared in open jeeps and entered the tent with Schwarzkopf and the commanders of the Saudi, British, and French forces.

After the two-hour private meeting, Schwarzkopf shook hands with and saluted the Iraqi generals. The Allied commander told reporters that he was "very happy to tell you that we agreed on all matters." The Saudi commander added that the Iraqis had been willing "not only to answer, but to satisfy us in every request we had." The most important term agreed upon was the release of Allied prisoners. Within three days, the Iraqis released all the Allied POWs they held to the Red Cross. Another cease-fire term called for Allied and Iraqi forces to avoid contact. This would reduce tension between the armies and make incidents leading to further violence less likely. The agreement also demanded that the Iraqis provide information about the location of their explosive

After being released from Iraqi custody, a group of POWs is led to Red Cross vehicles waiting to take them to freedom.

land mines in Kuwait. Without this information, finding and destroying Iraqi land mines would be a random, dangerous process. Many Allied soldiers and Kuwaiti citizens might be killed.

Iraq Torn by Civil Strife

As the United States and the Allies completed the terms of the cease-fire, new fighting erupted in Iraq. The war had significantly weakened Saddam's army and disrupted the government's communications and transportation networks. Some Iraqi citizens who opposed Saddam's brutal dictatorship saw their chance to topple him. They formed rebel groups and attacked units of Saddam's army. Many times during the Gulf crisis, President Bush had called upon the Iraqi people to rise up and overthrow Saddam. This convinced the Iraqi rebels that American troops would help them in their struggle.

On March 6, 1991, only days after the Gulf War cease-fire, Iraqi rebels in several southern cities rose in rebellion. In Basra, the fighting was especially bloody and chaotic. Some Iraqi soldiers joined the rebels and fired their tanks into a huge portrait of Saddam as bloody street fighting engulfed the city. Rebels stormed the local prison and released the prisoners, most of whom had been jailed for opposing the government.

The unrest quickly spread to other sections of Iraq. In the northern part of the country, tens of thousands of Kurds, members of Iraq's largest ethnic group, engaged in guerrilla warfare with Iraqi army units. The Kurds have language and customs very different from other Iraqis and had been demanding their own homeland for decades. The Kurds had rebelled once before, in the 1960s. Since that time, Iraqi leaders, including Saddam, had treated the Kurds harshly. In the 1980s, Saddam destroyed some five thousand

Iraqi Kurds flee to neighboring Turkey to escape persecution by the Iraqi army.

Kurdish villages, leaving the survivors homeless and starving. In 1988, he unleashed chemical weapons on a Kurdish town, killing more than five thousand people and forcing hundreds of thousands of Kurds to flee to Turkey and Iran. Now the remaining Iraqi Kurds believed their chance to break free of Saddam's rule had finally come.

For more than two weeks, the Kurds and other rebels fought Saddam's troops in many sections of the country. But by late March, the tide began to turn in the government's favor. Iraqi attack helicopters launched devastating raids on crowds of civilians as well as rebel fighters. A visiting Egyptian witnessed Saddam's troops slaughtering civilians in the town of Karbala. The visitor recalled how, for three days, "It was nothing but killing, killing, killing."

As crippled rebel forces retreated, they constantly asked, "Where are the Americans?" and "Why has Bush forsaken us?" Some members of the U.S. Congress criticized the president for not helping the rebels after encouraging them to revolt. Bush responded that the U.N.-sponsored goal of the Allies was to liberate Kuwait, not to get involved in Iraq's internal troubles. But according to the Iraqi rebels, it was the war that had sparked the rebellions in the first place. They were risking their lives, they said, to overthrow Saddam as the Americans had urged. Now the Americans had abandoned them. Many Westerners felt that the U.S. failure to help the rebels constituted a stain on the otherwise shining victory of Desert Storm.

By late April 1991, Saddam's troops had crushed the rebellion. An estimated two million Kurds had fled their homes for the mountains of northern Iraq. The refugees, camped on rough, muddy hillsides with little food and no fresh water, died at the rate of at least a thousand a day. Relief efforts by the member countries of the United Nations did not bring enough food and medical supplies fast enough. American, British, and other Allied troops patrolled some northern towns and tried to get the Kurds to return to their homes. But most of the refugees refused to return for fear of being massacred by Saddam's soldiers after the Allies left. When, after many weeks, the Allied patrols did leave, Kurdish leaders met with Saddam Hussein. They worked out a temporary cease-fire between rebel and government forces. Since that time, relations between the Kurds and the Iraqi government have been tense and uneasy, and the fate of the Kurds remains uncertain.

The Question of Arms and Security

The fate of the Kurds and the failure of the rebellion marred the otherwise brilliant Allied victory. In the wake of these events, Americans questioned other policies of the U.S. government. One of these policies was the sale of arms to Middle Eastern countries like Iraq. During the war, it was a supreme irony that much of the artillery lobbed at American forces was American and European made. France, Italy, the United States, the Soviet Union, and Germany, nations which opposed Iraq in the war, all sold Saddam arms in the 1980s. In a sense, the Allies defanged a monster they themselves helped create. One reason large, powerful countries sell weapons is that their economies depend heavily on arms sales. In France alone, for instance, 600,000 workers are employed by weapons makers. Another factor is large nations gain military allies by selling weapons. For example, the United States sold weapons to Saudi Arabia and other Middle Eastern nations in

An Iraqi woman washes out some clothing in a rain puddle while awaiting permission to enter Kuwait to escape the violent aftermath of the war.

hopes of persuading them to give less support to the Soviets and more to the United States.

Still another factor in arms sales is the attempt to either strengthen an ally or weaken an enemy. For decades, for instance, the United States supplied Israel with weapons to assure its security. Then, in the 1980s, the Americans armed Iraq, hoping Saddam would defeat Iran, a country at odds with the United States. These policies led to problems. For one thing, American military backing of Israel caused many Arabs to distrust the United States. And Saddam ended up using weapons from the United States and other Western countries to invade Kuwait and fight the Allies. It is unlikely that arms sales to small countries will stop in the future. However, the events of the Gulf War suggest that the United States and other powerful nations need to consider more carefully the risks and consequences of such sales.

Besides curbing arms sales, another factor in maintaining Middle East peace was providing the region with military security. After the war, President Bush announced that the United States would keep military personnel and equipment in Saudi Arabia, Kuwait, and the Persian Gulf for some time to come. This would help discourage Saddam or any other would-be aggressors in the region from attacking their neighbors. The Arabs would also provide security. Immediately after the cease-fire went into effect, Secretary James Baker traveled to seven Middle Eastern countries in eleven days. He tried to convince the leaders of these nations to form a Middle Eastern security force to prevent future wars in the area. The countries of the region would supply economic backing, and the United States would provide sea and air support.

The Quest for Peace

While building security and curbing arms sales are essential to maintaining peace in the Middle East, international cooperation is also important. One of the most dramatic and significant aspects of the Persian Gulf War was the peace-keeping role played by the United Nations. For the first time since its creation in 1945, the U.N. had taken a firm and militarily successful stand against aggression. Commented American journalist Mark Whitaker, "The most positive diplomatic lesson to emerge from the war against Saddam is that international police forces can work.... Now there's hopeful talk about making this kind of cooperation permanent."

People around the world were hopeful that the action taken by the U.N.-backed Allies would serve notice to other dictators. The message: Aggression will be instantly condemned and dealt with forcefully. This does not necessarily mean that the U.N. will always be able to prevent aggressions and other conflicts. But the actions taken by the U.N. during the Gulf War constitute an important step toward a more peaceful future for all nations.

Glossary

air superiority complete control of the sky above a given region.

amphibious assault an attack from, in, or over water.

annex officially add a territory to an existing state.

atrocity act of unusual violence and cruelty.

biological attack warfare using germs to infect the enemy.

coalition an alliance.

colonial empire a group of colonies administered by a country.

convoy an assembly of trucks, tanks, ships, or other vehicles.

embargo an order restricting trade.

guerrilla warfare informal fighting using methods such as ambush and harassment.

jihad in Islam, a holy war.

linkage relating or equating one topic with another.

mandate the right of one country to govern another; also, the authority to act when backed by a majority of the people.

mobilization the assembly of people and equipment, as in a war or emergency.

pan-Arab composed of or affecting all Arabs.

paratrooper a soldier who jumps with a parachute from an airplane.

pilgrimage a journey.

POW prisoner of war.

range effective traveling distance of a weapon.

resolution a negotiated rule or proposal.

revelation a religious message given to a human by God.

sanction penalty, usually economic in nature.

sortie an individual mission or raid.

strategy military or other planning.

tactician one who is skilled in military tactics.

tactics in warfare, the art of achieving a specific goal.

For Further Reading

Author's note: For up-to-date information and breaking stories from the Middle East, the *New York Times,* the *Wall Street Journal, Time, Newsweek,* and *U.S. News & World Report* provide excellent coverage. The following sources offer good general overviews of some of the topics covered in this book.

R. Arias, "As War Claims Its First Female M.I.A., Melissa Rathbun-Nealy's Pals Recall One Tough, Spirited Kid," *People Weekly,* February 18, 1991.

John Barry and Evan Thomas, "A Textbook Victory," *Newsweek,* March 11, 1991.

Mary Louise Clifford, *The Land and People of the Arabian Peninsula.* New York: J.B. Lippincott, 1977.

David C. Cooke, *Kuwait, Miracle in the Desert.* New York: Grosset and Dunlap, 1970.

Editors of the Encyclopaedia Britannica, *The Arabs: People and Power.* New York: Bantam Books, 1978.

Caesar E. Farah, *Islam: Beliefs and Observances.* New York: Barron's, 1987.

Charles Lane, "Arms for Sale," *Newsweek,* April 8, 1991.

Gary E. McCuen, *Iran-Iraq War.* Hudson, WI: G.E.M. Publications, 1987.

Dan McKinnon, *Bullseye Iraq* (story of Israeli raid that destroyed Saddam Hussein's atomic bomb factory). New York: Berkley Books, 1987.

Tom Morganthau and Russell Watson, "Allied Blitzkreig," *Newsweek,* March 4, 1991.

Time, "Combat in the Sand," February 11, 1991.

U.S. News & World Report, "The Gulf War," February 18, 1991.

Russell Watson, "Baghdad's Bully," *Newsweek,* August 13, 1990.

World Press Review, "Saddam vs. the World," October, 1990.

Works Consulted

R. W. Apple, "Devil of a War," *New York Times,* January 27, 1991.

Aviation Week and Space Technology, "Persian Gulf Crisis Four Months Later," December 3, 1990.

M. Barone, "The End of the Vietnam Syndrome," *U.S. News & World Report,* August 20, 1990.

M. Barone and D. Gergen, "The Building War Scenario," *U.S. News & World Report,* October 15, 1990.

J. Bierman and B. Levin, "The Hostages in the Gulf," *Maclean's,* August 27, 1990.

Business Week, "The Gulf War," February 11, 1991.

H. G. Chua-Eoan, "Strains on the Coalition," *Time,* December 10, 1990.

Daniel C. Diller, ed., *The Middle East.* Washington, DC: *Congressional Quarterly,* 1990.

M. Dugan, "The Air War," *U.S. News & World Report,* February 11, 1991.

Col. Trevor M. Dupuy et al, *How to Defeat Saddam Hussein: Scenarios and Strategies for the Gulf War.* New York: Warner Books, 1991.

T. Fennell, "The High-tech Battlefront," *Maclean's,* January 28, 1991.

M. S. Forbes, "Postwar Prosperity and Peace in the Middle East," *Forbes,* February 18, 1991.

Thomas Friedman and Patrick Tyler, "From the First, U.S. Resolve to Fight," *New York Times,* March 3, 1991.

Michael Gordon, "Outnumbered and Outgunned, Allied Forces Outfox Hussein," *New York Times,* February 28, 1991.

D.H. Hackworth, "Life with the Line Doggies: Saddam's Suicidal Assault on Kafji," *Newsweek,* February 11, 1991.

J. Howse, "An Uncertain Christmas," *Maclean's,* November 26, 1990.

J. D. Hull, "Fear and Loathing in Israel," *Time,* October 8, 1990.

J. B. Kelly, "America, the Gulf and the West," *National Review,* October 15, 1990.

J. Leo, "Protesting a Complex War," *U.S. News & World Report,* February 4, 1991.

Bernard Lewis, *The Arabs in History.* New York: Harper & Row Publishers, 1958.

T. Masland, "A Tide of Terrorism," *Newsweek,* February 18, 1991.

Judith Miller and Laurie Mylroie, *Saddam Hussein and the Crisis in the Gulf.* New York: New York Times Books, 1990.

Tom Morganthau, "The Military's New Image," *Newsweek,* March 11, 1991.

The New York Times, "Excerpts from Schwarzkopf News Conference on Gulf War," February 28, 1991.

The New York Times, "Iraqis Surrender to Italian TV," February 28, 1991.

Jean P. Sasson, *The Rape of Kuwait: The True Story of Iraqi Atrocities Against a Civilian Population.* New York: Knightsbridge Publishing, 1991.

John Schwartz, "The Mind of a Missile," *Newsweek,* February 18, 1991.

K. R. Sheets, "Iraq's Environmental Warfare," *U.S. News & World Report,* February 4, 1991.

Evan Thomas and John Barry, "War's New Science," *Newsweek,* February 18, 1991.

Time, "The Fog of War," February 4, 1991.

Time, "Iraq's Power Grab," August 13, 1990.

Russell Watson, "Desert Victory: After the Storm," *Newsweek,* March 11, 1991.

World Press Review, "Saddam Hussein Changes the Gulf Equation," September 1990.

Index

Abbas, Abu, 42
Africa, 13
Apache helicopter, 48, 60-61, 79
Arab-Israeli wars, 16-17, 19
Arab League, 15, 28
  criticism of Hussein, 40, 41
  war against Israel, 16-17
Arabs
  alliance with Soviets, 17, 19
  British and French promises to, 11
  efforts to unite, 14-15, 23
  opposed to Iraqi invasion, 40, 63
  resentment toward Westerners, 11-12, 14, 20
  support for Hussein, 22, 41, 52
  traditional life-style of, 9
  wars against Israel, 16, 17, 19
arms sales, 88-89
Arnett, Peter, 55
Aziz, Tarik, 28, 44, 52

Ba'athist party, 23, 25
Babylonian Empire, 23
Baker, James, 32, 49, 50
  career of, 51
  negotiation efforts of, 52, 89
Balfour Declaration, 12
Beck, Melinda, 80
Bedouins, 27
Ben-Gurion, David, 16
Bush, George, 8
  career of, 35
  during Gulf crisis
    appeal to Congress, 52
    decision to oppose Iraq, 36-37, 45
    decision to start ground war, 69, 70
    plan to invade Kuwait, 49-50
    plea to Israel, 63
    policy goals of, 38
    sanctions against Iraq, 30-31
    Iraq's nuclear research and, 46
    Kurdish rebellion and, 86, 87
    victory announcement of, 81
  popular support for, 83
  reaction to Iraq's seizure of Westerners, 43-44

Canada, 49
chemical weapons, 41, 46, 71

fear Iraq would use, 61, 63, 84
  in Iran-Iraq war, 21, 43
  used against Iraqis, 25
Christianity, 10
  Moslem beliefs about, 13
CIA (Central Intelligence Agency), 35
Clifton, Tony, 76-77
CNN (Cable News Network)
  reports of Baghdad bombing, 55, 60
colonialism, 14
computers, 59, 60, 65, 73
cruise missiles, 38, 59, 60
Crusades, 10
Cuba, 51

Desert Shield, Operation, 37, 50, 62, 80
  see also Persian Gulf War; Saudi Arabia
Desert Storm, Operation, 56, 61, 62, 80
  see also Persian Gulf War

Egypt
  during Suez Canal crisis, 18-19
  in Allied coalition, 63, 71
  reaction to Iraqi invasion, 40, 41
  wars against Israel, 19
environmental damage, 66, 82

Fahd, King, 39-40
Fitzwater, Marlin, 56
France, 10, 18, 53
  citizens of in Iraq and Kuwait, 43
  embassy in Kuwait, 44
  freeing of colonies, 14
  mandate in Syria, 12
  military sales to Iraq, 21, 24, 88
  participation in ground war, 71
  sanctions against Iraq, 30
  troops in Saudi Arabia, 47, 49

Geneva Protocol (1925), 41
Germany, 10, 11
  arms sales of, 88
  embassy in Kuwait, 44
  persecution of Jews, 15
Great Britain, 11
  arms sales of, 88
  citizens of in Iraq and Kuwait, 43-44

control of Middle East oil, 14
  during Suez Canal crisis, 18-19
  embassy in Kuwait, 44
  evacuation from Palestine, 16
  mandate in Middle East, 12, 15
  participation in war, 49, 60, 71
  sanctions against Iraq, 30

Hackworth, David H., 67
helicopters, 48, 60-61, 73, 79, 87
Herzl, Theodor, 12
Holliman, John, 55
hostages, Western, 43-44, 46
  freeing of, 49
Hussein, Saddam
  Arab support for, 22
  attack on Kafji, 67, 68
  attack on Kuwait
    annexation effort, 39
    order to close Kuwaiti embassies, 44
    reasons for, 26, 27
    warnings of, 28
    Western hostages, 43-44, 46
  career of, 25
  dictatorship of, 22, 23, 24, 25
    opposition to, 85, 86, 87
    persecution of Kurds, 86-87
  environmental terrorism, 66
  position after Iran-Iraq war, 21
  reaction to Desert Storm, 61, 69
  reaction to world pressure, 7, 31, 33, 34, 40, 45
  Schwarzkopf's assessment of, 82
  Scud attacks, 65
    on Israel, 61, 63
    on Saudi Arabia, 64, 66
  terrorism threat of, 42, 43, 61, 84
  U.S. failure to depose, 84-85
  Western arms sales to, 88, 89

Iran
  Arab opposition to, 24
  border disputes, 20
  Kurds in, 87
  war with Iraq, 21, 24
Iran-Iraq war, 21, 24, 41, 79
Iraq
  ancient culture of, 23
  annexation of Kuwait, 39
  arms sales to, 88-89
  Ba'ath party's role in, 23, 25

Photo Credits

Cover photo by Reuters/Bettmann

AP/Wide World Photos, 16, 17, 18 (both), 19 (both), 20, 25, 26, 27, 28, 29 (both), 31, 32, 35, 36 (both), 37 (both), 38 (left), 40 (both), 41, 42 (both), 49 (bottom), 50, 51, 54, 56, 57 (top), 59 (bottom), 60, 62, 63 (both), 65 (left), 66 (both), 67, 75 (both), 77, 78, 79, 80, 81 (right), 83, 84 (both), 85, 86, 87, 88

The Bettmann Archive, 10, 23, 58

Cable News Network, 55

Robert Coldwell, 57 (bottom), 59 (top), 65 (right)

David Puckett/Los Angeles Times. Copyright, 1991, Los Angeles Times. Reprinted by permission, 48, 73

Reuters/Bettmann, 7, 38 (right), 39 (both), 47 (both), 49 (top), 68, 69, 70, 71, 76, 81 (left)

Simon Wiesenthal Center, 15 (both)

UPI/Bettmann, 8

About the Author

Don Nardo is an actor, film director, and composer, as well as an award-winning writer. As an actor, he has appeared in more than fifty stage productions. He has also worked before or behind the camera in twenty films. Several of his musical compositions, including a young person's version of *The War of the Worlds* and the oratorio *Richard III,* have been played by regional orchestras. Mr. Nardo's writing credits include short stories, articles, and more than twenty-five books. Among his other writings are an episode of ABC's "Spenser: for Hire" and numerous screenplays. Mr. Nardo lives with his wife, Christine, on Cape Cod, Massachusetts.